the
gathering
place

Other books by Graham Kerr

Graham Kerr's Smart Cooking

Graham Kerr's Minimax ™ Cookbook

Graham Kerr's Creative Choices Cookbook

Graham Kerr's Kitchen

Graham Kerr's Best

Graham Kerr's Swiftly Seasoned

New York

Fort Lauderdale

St. Thomas

Colombia

Acapulco

Los Angeles

Ensenada

Kailua-Kona

Oahu

American Samoa

Fiji

New Zealand

Sydney

the gathering place

informal

international

menus

that bring

family

and

friends

back to the table

Graham Kerr

Food photography by David Burch
Travel photography by Treena Kerr
Tool photography by Jim Lippert

Camano Press

Camano Press
P. O. Box 1598
Stanwood, WA 98292

Photography props courtesy of:
Bon Marché - Seattle, WA
Festivities - Edmonds, WA
Go Outside - La Conner, WA
The Greenhouse - Bellingham, WA
Kong Lung Company - Kilauea, Kauai, HI
Mrs. Cooks - Seattle, WA
Sur La Table - Seattle, WA

Book design:
Bunkhouse Studio - Fir Island, WA

Library of Congress Catalog Card Number: 97-68990
ISBN 0-9657606-0-X
Manufactured in the United States of America
2 4 6 8 10 9 7 5 3 1
Distributed to the trade by Publishers Group West

To my son and publisher,
Andrew Ian Robert Kerr.

Years ago, I pushed you out in a small boat.
Now, it's your turn.
Enjoy the journey!

Acknowledgments

Just like a wonderful meal in a fine restaurant, a book involves many talented people who are devoted to the creative process and an excellent final product. In developing this book for you, I have been blessed to have the support and friendship of many creative people. If they were to be presented to you in menu form, the epicurean lineup might read:

Appetizers and Starters

Treena Kerr
Head Critic and Travel Photographer
Thoughtful guidance with flowery overtones of grace and femininity.

Andy Kerr
Publisher and President, Kerr Corporation
Boldly going where no other family member has gone before.

David Matthews
Friend and Advisor
Unique southern charm enhanced with thoughtful advice.

Suzanne Thostenson
Senior Food Associate
A creative palate for the lingering flavors of friendship.

Chef Rudi Sodaman
Executive Chef, Cunard Lines
Undertones of great style gleaned from sailing the seven seas.

Vegetarian Option
Kristine Duncan
Registered Dietitian and Secretary
Abundant dedication and appreciation for food, facts, and plants.

Entrées and Main Dishes

Kris Molesworth
Senior Editor and Project Coordinator
Clear, concise and full of creative vision.

Susan Hughes-Hayton
Designer
Acute eye and balanced sensibility.

Claire Beckham Nisbet
Copy Editor
Infinite attention to detail and dedication to meaning.

Side Dishes

David Burch
Photographer
Full of warm and glowing English light.

Karin Rowles
Office Manager
Outgoing nature wrapped in caring and delight.

Julie MacIntosh
Advance Researcher
Fresh every day with bright notes and clear insights.

Desserts

American Dietetic Association
Healthfilled, responsive, and glowing with information.

Culinary Institute of America
Revitalizing and refreshing, layered with texture and excitement.

Skagit Valley College
Effervescent enthusiasm and tasty support.

Relishes

Jan Fekkes, Michaeline Lancaster,
Lisa Ekus and Merrilyn Lewis, Heather Cameron,
and Tessa Kerr.

table of contents

Introduction

Why The Gathering Place?

I passionately believe that the home dining table is our last remaining tribal gathering place. Sitting face-to-face, elbow-to-elbow over hot, steaming plates of simple food, we nourish our bodies and feed our souls. This is the place where families and friends gather. A place where communities take shape and hospitality beckons. A place where self-worth is fostered. And a place where tender feelings and ruffled feathers can be soothed simply by breaking bread together.

As I sort through a lifetime of memories, I find that many of them center around a table. Some of these tables were lavishly laid, in exotic places that Treena and I visited during years of travel and television. Other tables were quite humble, simply the sharing of daily bread by generous friends who had very little. Some tables hosted the family celebrations that mark the passing of time and raising of children: birthdays, anniversaries, and homecomings.

But as I examine more recent memories, I discover that we have drifted away from the table during the past few years, a trend that I believe many of us share. For awhile, television news tempted us to balance trays on our knees and fret about world events while we ate. Busy schedules meant that eating often became snacking, and hospitality seemed like too much work.

I first began to consider this during the time that Treena and I were producing the "Galloping Gourmet" television series, one of the busiest periods of our life together. We lived in Ottawa, Canada, in a lovely vintage residence located in the Rockcliffe Park area. We were a long way from our home in Sydney, Australia and without a stick of furniture. In search of furnishings to fill our large dining room, we happened across a grand dining set that once belonged to the King of Norway. [Ottawa is a diplomatic center, which made for quite interesting shopping!] Carved from oak and upholstered in rich damask, the twelve-seater seemed made for the room. We went on to buy Spode china, Sheffield silver cutlery, Waterford crystal glasses, and a baker's dozen of everything. The fabulous table glittered and twinkled in the candlelight...surrounded by lots of empty chairs. The trouble was, we were too busy to sit down at that table. Here I was, the champion of the creative kitchen, and I didn't have the time to cook for anyone in my own home! We had lots of good intentions, of course, but simply seemed to have no time in our schedule to gather with friends.

During the past few years, I have traveled a good deal, moving out of the television studio and into settings with live audiences. Whenever I lecture, I always ask the folks in the audience how often they have hosted people in their home for a meal during the past year. Given my own experience, I am not surprised at the response I receive. We have simply convinced ourselves that we are too busy to entertain, even in casual, informal ways. Now, I won't pretend that I have a scientific statistical survey to prove these findings, but think about it. When was the last time you had a few friends in for a casual dinner in your home simply for the joy of being together? In fact, while I'm at it, let me ask you a few more personal questions: Are you waiting to finish fixing up the kitchen or purchase new china before you entertain? Do you feel that dinner parties require high standards and your best recipes? Do you hesitate to make dates ahead of time because you want to stay flexible in case you have a tough week at work? Have you recently decided to change the way you eat; say, reduce the amount of harmful fats in your diet, and you worry that dinner with friends would be too rich?

These are the kinds of concerns that led me to write *The Gathering Place*. In one way or another, I've had many of the same feelings. Concerns about my time, my schedule, and my eating habits have often caused me to miss opportunities to be with friends and experience the fun that those times can bring. Now I'm devoted to finding creative, healthy ways to bring us all back to the table.

Remember Gourmet Clubs?

The "Galloping Gourmet" television series began in 1969 and seemed to coincide with lots of interest in gourmet dinner parties. I happened along at just the right time with a popular message that encouraged people to have fun in the kitchen. You didn't have to jump over a chair with a wine glass, as I often did; you just had to relax and see what happened. Millions of people decided to "give it a go," and many of them formed gourmet clubs, or circles of friends that met regularly to enjoy interesting new food and wine. The concept was for several friends to gather and try new foods, experiment with ethnic dishes, or plan international theme evenings. Each person brought a different dish, like an upscale potluck. The clubs worked because the attitude was relaxed and fun and seemed to do away with the fear of failure as well as desire to compete! During the eighties and nineties, however, gourmet clubs began to dwindle. Workloads increased, children had busy schedules, and corporate downsizing sharpened our competitive instincts.

The flickering light of televisions and blinking digital screens cast their spell, and many family meals began to take place within an electronic setting.

Supermarkets and fast food chains immediately spotted this trend and helped us spend less and less time cooking. In fact, there's an industrial acronym for a new generation of foodstuffs: HMRs, or home meal replacements. I began to ponder the fate of cooking from scratch: would it become a charming handicraft, like quilting or putting up apricot preserves? Call me an optimist, but I don't believe so. I've simply met too many people during the past few years who are longing to putter around in the kitchen, gather with friends, and enjoy the healthy fellowship of the table. Time is a problem, certainly. However, I'm convinced there are pockets of time that can be wisely invested in the caring, casual preparation of special meals for friends. Perhaps this will only take place on weekends, but I believe our need to be together will lead us back to the table and into the next century.

A Healthy New Twist

My goal is to inspire you to make casual gatherings part of your life again, but with a few twists. Given the things we have learned about nutrition in the last decade, we need to search for variety "on the lighter side." Millions of us have been advised by our physicians to change our eating habits in order to enjoy better health. Perhaps your doctor has suggested you reduce the amount of saturated fat you eat. Or maybe you're working hard to lose a few stubborn pounds. Often a health challenge such as diabetes causes concern and makes entertaining a challenge. I urge you, in your journey toward good health, not to take a detour around entertaining. The benefits of fellowship and communal dining can enhance your health and well-being in ways that a bowl of lentils, enjoyed alone, can never do.

Now, I know that we are often tempted to set aside the rules of healthy eating and make an exception when it comes to entertaining. "It's a special occasion!" I am just as convinced that we can use casual dinners with friends to enjoy healthy foods with exciting flavors without the excessive use of fat, sugar, or salt. In fact, sharing new recipes with friends can often lead to changes in our day-to-day cooking as we creatively try to meet the health needs of our loved ones. By searching internationally for food and flavors, we can add many new tastes from faraway lands.

Our Voyage on the Queen Elizabeth II

In 1996, my wife Treena and I were invited to join the crew and passengers of the Cunard Lines' Queen Elizabeth II, one of the world's largest, fastest, and most famous all-weather cruise ships. Our only obligation was to share our philosophy of healthy eating and balanced lifestyles in a series of seminars presented on board during a voyage that would take us halfway around the world.

The journey was illuminating in a number of ways. First, we met hundreds of people who were deeply interested in making healthful changes in their lives but didn't want to give up socializing with friends. Second, at each port Treena and I visited markets, cafés, and private homes, exploring the native foods, flavors, and ingredients of different cultures. We would disembark early and return late. We searched for the true, unique flavors and foods enjoyed by the people of each country for all kinds of climatic and cultural reasons. As we sailed back to the United States, I realized we had collected more than ethnic recipes; we were bringing home a collection of feelings as well. We had identified many different tastes, interesting ingredients, new techniques, and textures that could be used at home to bring the flavors of the world to our own healthful table. This is what I bring to you in *The Gathering Place*.

Reflecting on our Journey

As I set about developing a book based on our journey, I tried to create dishes that were not pale reflections of their classic namesakes, but new recipes that pay homage to their history and branch out into the future. I was looking for new tastes from other lands that could marry with more familiar tastes, textures, and aromas that we already love in order to create new favorites. In many cases I took recipes for famous traditional dishes and "springboarded" them into formats using less fats, salt, and sugar. Other recipes are based on entirely new ideas using ingredients and techniques that are unique to different cultures.

A Reasonable Framework

Imagine, if you will, a nicely presented picture. There's a frame, then a generous mat that separates the picture from its frame. I'd like to propose that the frame is the outer limit within which you design a healthy meal. For instance, most people can easily enjoy a festive dinner that has less than 1,000 calories and about 20% of calories from fat. Others, like my wife Treena, have special needs and only 10% of those calories should be from fat. Whatever the size of your frame, use it as a guideline in developing meals you enjoy. Then use the mat as a flexible area in which to make playful changes or adaptations. Perhaps you'd like to add a little cream or a bit of wine to a certain recipe. There's plenty of room to do that within the framework of this book without moving out of the healthy guidelines you have set for yourself.

How to Use This Book

This book is arranged as a series of thirteen dinners, each based around a different port of call. Each menu includes an appetizer, main course, vegetable side dish, and dessert. I have provided vegetarian options for all dishes that contain meat. The dinners are designed to yield six servings, a very nice size for a dinner party, although you can modify the recipes for any combination of guests. In addition, each recipe can stand alone on other occasions and be used in other menus on a mix-and-match basis. The menus can also be used as a format for a family dinner with eleven or twelve-year-old children given the appetizer or the dessert to prepare.

The first element of planning is to pick a chapter, or a country, for the occasion. You may choose to follow along on our voyage or strike out on your own. Whatever you choose, it makes sense to plan ahead, perhaps as long as a month, as you may need to do a bit of special shopping for this culinary adventure. [I've provided some help to locate unusual foods in most chapters.]

Next, invite your friends and let them choose the course they would like to bring. Perhaps at your first party you could draw names for future assignments. The host makes the main dish, arranges the table, and offers appropriate beverages. The other guests bring the appetizer and the dessert, which I have designed to be especially portable. Also, I've worked hard to keep the prep time to thirty minutes or less, so everything should be "do-able" on the afternoon of the party.

How to Plan for Your Party

If you're like me, even a casual dinner with friends takes some planning in order to find the time. In fact, when I get my new diary, usually in December, Treena and I mark up at least ten Saturdays as "gatherings" and then propose these dates to our friends. After a bit of maneuvering, we usually settle on eight or ten dates that work for all of us.

size of your frame, use it as a guideline in developing meals you enjoy. Then use the mat as a flexible area in which to make playful changes or adaptations. Perhaps you'd like to add a little cream or a bit of wine to a certain recipe. There's plenty of room to do that within the framework of this book without moving out of the healthy guidelines you have set for yourself.

How to Use This Book

This book is arranged as a series of thirteen dinners, each based around a different port of call. Each menu includes an appetizer, main course, vegetable side dish, and dessert. I have provided vegetarian options for all dishes that contain meat. The dinners are designed to yield six servings, a very nice size for a dinner party, although you can modify the recipes for any combination of guests. In addition, each recipe can stand alone on other occasions and be used in other menus on a mix-and-match basis. The menus can also be used as a format for a family dinner with eleven or twelve-year-old children given the appetizer or the dessert to prepare.

The first element of planning is to pick a chapter, or a country, for the occasion. You may choose to follow along on our voyage or strike out on your own. Whatever you choose, it makes sense to plan ahead, perhaps as long as a month, as you may need to do a bit of special shopping for this culinary adventure. [I've provided some help to locate unusual foods in most chapters.]

Next, invite your friends and let them choose the course they would like to bring. Perhaps at your first party you could draw names for future assignments. The host makes the main dish, arranges the table, and offers appropriate beverages. The other guests bring the appetizer and the dessert, which I have designed to be especially portable. Also, I've worked hard to keep the prep time to thirty minutes or less, so everything should be "do-able" on the afternoon of the party.

How to Plan for Your Party

If you're like me, even a casual dinner with friends takes some planning in order to find the time. In fact, when I get my new diary, usually in December, Treena and I mark up at least ten Saturdays as "gatherings" and then propose these dates to our friends. After a bit of maneuvering, we usually settle on eight or ten dates that work for all of us.

When you set a date, assure your friends that no dressing up, either of oneself or the table, is required. What is important about these gatherings is that they bring people together who are loved for who they are. Regardless of your china, linen, or the construction stage of your remodeling project, the point is to enjoy each others' company in a fun and casual atmosphere. And please do not feel like you have to test the recipes beforehand; I've taken care of that. Preparing these dishes for the first time with friends only enhances the fun!

About Special Ingredients

While Thai fish sauce may seem strange to you in the midwestern United States, please remember that ketchup is a pretty odd condiment in Bangkok! I bring this up because you may find a number of ingredients that seem a little unusual as you flip through these recipes. I very much enjoy exploring the world of flavors, and I believe that many of these "new" ingredients can creatively take the place of the excessive fat, oil, salt, sugar, and large portions of meat protein that prove so harmful in our diets. Part of the fun of this whole idea is that you slowly begin to accumulate some special seasonings and flavorings that you've never tried before. When these ingredients are in your pantry, you tend to use them during the week to bring fresh new tastes to some very familiar dishes.

I was recently browsing through a gigantic supermarket, accompanied by the company's president. An elderly lady stopped him to ask for a special ingredient and he went out of his way to find it for her. When I took note of his concern, he explained: "An average customer spends between $4,000 and $8,000 a year in this store. They deserve to find what they need, and I have a lot to lose if they don't." So do be straightforward and ask for what you need. If you're unable to find a special ingredient in your community, you'll find help within these pages. We've tried to track down sources for every single ingredient that might not be in your corner supermarket. These are listed with the suppliers' customer service numbers and addresses so that you can either ask your supermarket to order for you or place your order directly with the supplier.

A thoughtful gift of friendship would be to buy extra packages of any unusual ingredient used in the meal and share them with the other guests. That way, the gift of seasoning goes to each home to enhance many more meals.

About Beverages

As a good host, I believe that everyone should be helped to feel at home, and if this means that wine is to be served for some and tea for others, then let both be selected for the best of balance and enjoyment without a single sidelong glance. I'm certainly not going to begin a whole dissertation on wine, largely because I decided some years ago to look for creative alternatives for those of us who really enjoy good food and good company, but for all manner of reasons prefer not to consume alcohol. Having said that, I must now make one qualification. It might be that one of your dear friends is a recovering alcoholic who may well find it extremely difficult to be at ease whilst everyone else is happily celebrating with a great cabernet sauvignon. One solution is to serve a delicious tea or fruit-based drink for everyone. Another solution is to serve one of the *better* dealcoholized wines being made nowadays. These wines are made exactly as the art demands, then filtered by reverse osmosis to remove the alcohol. A few of them have won gold medals in competitions where they were placed side-by-side with conventional wines. It must be said that these are not wines, but neither are they grape juices. Like any grape product, some are excellent and some are just plain bad, so please be selective.

Gather in Good Health

I hope that as you voyage through *The Gathering Place*, you will find the rewards of gathering with your friends in a healthful, creative way. Many of us are seeking change toward a healthy lifestyle. If the journey is creative, and the process enjoyable, I believe lasting change can be achieved. And where better to start than at your own dining table? Enjoy...and God bless.

salad
Union Square Summer Salad
*Ripened tomatoes and fresh, sweet corn sprinkled with
a balsamic vinegar sauce.*

main course
Greenwich Village Potato and Onion Tart
*A MEV formed with a garbanzo bean custard and topped with
a rosemary glaze.*

vegetable
Broiled Tomatoes

dessert
Blintzes with Strawberries
*Delicate pancakes filled with smooth yogurt cheese and dried strawberries;
fresh strawberry garnish.*

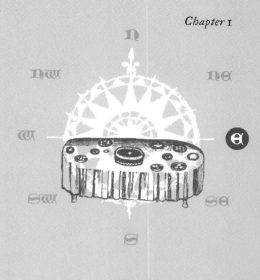

travelogue

*A*lthough many modern cruises now leave from Florida in
order to avoid the rough waters off Cape Hatteras, Treena and I
made a sentimental decision to embark from New York City. Any
fan of old movies knows that a *real* ocean voyage must begin in
New York. I could picture the scene, complete with streamers
streaming and bands playing. We would recline in teak deck chairs
surrounded by attentive stewards bearing fine woolen blankets and
steaming cups of beef consommé. The grandeur of the Manhattan
skyline would rise behind the Queen Elizabeth II's gleaming red
smokestack and the Statue of Liberty would bid us farewell...just
like Barbara Stanwyck and Henry Fonda in *The Lady Eve.*

We arrived in New York a few days early so we could spend time
leisurely exploring one of our favorite cities. Ever since we first
came to the States, Treena and I have had a love affair with this
great city of contrasts and unexpected surprises. One of the
surprises that I discovered several years ago and revisit whenever
I'm in town is the Greenmarket at Union Square. There is a special
charm to a farmers' market amidst the crowded buildings and busy

NEW YORK
Urban Abundance...on the Lighter Side

streets of a big metropolis, something irresistible about squeezing vine-ripened tomatoes and pinching fresh corn in the open air. The vivid colors and fresh smells mix with the friendly banter of vendors to lend a festive air.

Located on the north side of historic Union Square, the Greenmarket was started in 1976 as a way for small farmers to protect their livelihood by selling directly to consumers. The

The market's vivid colors and fresh smells mix with the friendly banter of vendors to lend a festive air.

enthusiasm of the growers for this experiment proved contagious, and the market grew in both size and variety. Four days a week during the growing season, farmers and other food producers bring in an array of homegrown products from outlying rural areas. In addition to stalls mounded with an amazing assortment of fresh-picked fruits and vegetables, there are baked goods, honey, cider, cheeses, fish, meat, cut flowers, and much more. The council that oversees the market makes sure that there are no middlemen or brokers here, only bona fide regional growers who understand the value of meeting customers face-to-face. A wonderful side effect of the market's success has been the rejuvenation of the surrounding area. The once crime-ridden park has been cleaned up and reclaimed by residents, while old buildings around the perimeter of the square are continually being renovated as new businesses move into the revitalized neighborhood.

Previous page:
Filming the Greenmarket at Union Square.

This page, from top:
The Statue of Liberty bids us farewell as the QE II nudges her way out of New York Harbor.
First on-board filming in the Queen's Grill.

Facing page, from top:
Treena dresses for dinner our first night at sea.
Our professional waitstaff became our friends.
Our first taste of QE II fare.

After the hustle and bustle of the market, it is a pleasant stroll south through the tree-lined oasis of Union Square and into Greenwich Village, site of the rural hamlet that gave this area its name. The ground where farms and country retreats flourished a mere two centuries ago now sprouts a bountiful crop of bars, coffee houses, bookstores, art galleries, shops, and cafés of every imaginable persuasion.

I was in the Village to meet Leslie McEachern and visit Angelica Kitchen, her vegetarian restaurant located at 300 East 12th Street. Leslie is devoted to a concept I call FABIS, for "fresh and best in season." She and two talented chefs, Peter Berley and Myra Kornfeld, rely on seasonal produce to create healthy meals that are satisfying and full of robust flavor. After tasting fifteen of their most popular dishes, I begged them to open a restaurant near my

home in the Pacific Northwest. They politely declined, saying they prefer to do a small thing and do it very well. Until they change their minds, I'll have to travel to New York City to enjoy their wonderful cooking.

After one more afternoon in the city, Treena and I boarded the QE II to embark on our eighty-seven day odyssey. Our leave-taking was not quite as theatrical as I had envisioned, but we did get a farewell wave from the Statue of Liberty. As we slipped out of the Hudson River into the Atlantic Ocean, carrying with us more fond memories of New York and a pocketful of recipes from Angelica Kitchen, I was already thinking of a dinner to commemorate our visit.

The menu I came up with focuses on fresh fruits and vegetables, beginning with a tomato fan appetizer, followed by a potato and onion tart as entrée, and strawberry blintzes [of course!] for dessert.

As we slipped out of the Hudson River ... carrying with us more fond memories of New York and a pocketful of recipes from Angelica Kitchen, I was already thinking of a dinner to commemorate our visit.

Enjoy this vegetarian supper with friends on a warm summer evening when corn and tomatoes and strawberries are at the peak of the season. Serve a sparkling New York cider or chilled chardonnay [dealcoholized if you prefer] with the first two courses to enhance all those luxurious flavors straight from the garden. This entire meal [minus drinks] contains just over 700 calories and only 9 grams of fat, so you won't have to worry about making up for any indulgence after this.

Union Square Summer Salad
Tomato and Sweet Corn with Balsamic Sauce

Any farmers' market worth its salt will have an array of vine-ripened tomatoes as its cornerstone during the summer months. Handily, they come into peak season along with leaf basil and sweet corn—"fresh and best in season." This easily managed appetizer makes the perfect beginning for a summer supper.

SERVES 6

Salad

- 2-3 ears fresh corn, shucked
- 3 large ripe tomatoes

Balsamic Sauce

- 1/4 cup unsweetened apple juice
- 2 tablespoons balsamic vinegar
- 3/4 teaspoon arrowroot

Garnish

- 9 large basil leaves
- 6 fresh basil sprigs

To Prepare the Salad

1. Drop the ears of corn into a pot of rapidly boiling water and cook for 5 minutes. Remove from the heat and immediately immerse in ice water to chill. When cool enough to handle, cut the kernels from the cobs. Discard the cobs and refrigerate the kernels.

2. Core the tomatoes by cutting a shallow cone around the stem. Cut each tomato in half lengthwise, top to bottom, and lay the halves, cut side down, on a cutting board. With a sharp knife held parallel to the cutting board, cut thin slices across the tomato from the blossom end toward the stem end, stopping just before you cut all the way through. Make about six slices, discarding the top slice that is completely covered with skin. Repeat with all six tomato halves and set aside until ready to serve.

3. Combine the apple juice, vinegar, and arrowroot in a small saucepan. Stir over medium-high heat until the sauce thickens and turns glossy. Set aside to cool.

To Serve

4. Scatter the corn on individual salad plates. Lay a tomato half in the center of each plate and press down gently to fan out the slices. Drizzle about 1 tablespoon of the sauce over each tomato. Slice the basil leaves into thin strips and sprinkle over the corn and tomato. Lay a sprig of basil at the base of each tomato fan.

Time Estimate

Hands-on, 25 minutes.

Nutritional Profile per Serving

39 calories; 0 g fat; 0 g saturated fat; 4% of calories from fat; 10 g carbohydrate; 1 g dietary fiber.

Portability

Prepare the sauce ahead and carry it in a small plastic container. The tomatoes may be cut and carried in a flat plastic container. The corn kernels travel best in a resealable bag. The basil is easily bruised, so protect it in a rigid container and cut the leaves just before you serve the salad.

Greenwich Village Potato and Onion Tart

This terrific vegetable tart topped with a rosemary glaze was one of the recipes I brought home from Angelica Kitchen. The wonderful combination of potatoes and caramelized onions is held together by a soft, luscious chickpea "custard." The tart can be made in a deep quiche plate or pie tin, but I use my MEV pan for a neat, attractive presentation [see Tools, page 211]. This dish is a nice way to get acquainted with the MEV concept, which I hope will be useful to you in many different ways. Serve the tart with a side dish of Broiled Tomatoes [page 28].

SERVES 6

Chickpea Custard
- 6 cups cold water
- 2 cups chickpea flour*
- 1/2 teaspoon salt
- 1/4 teaspoon white pepper
  Pinch of powdered saffron*
- 1/2 teaspoon Poland Ethmix*
- 1 teaspoon fresh lemon juice
- 2 teaspoons capers

Onion and Potato Layer
- 1 teaspoon light olive oil
- 1 pound [450 g] sweet onions, cut into 1/2-inch [11/2-cm] dice [about 3 cups]
- 1/2 teaspoon caraway seeds
- 1 pound [450 g] Yellow Finn* or other waxy yellow potatoes, peeled and sliced 1/4-inch [3/4-cm] thick
- 1/8 teaspoon salt
- 1/4 teaspoon freshly ground black pepper
- 1 teaspoon white wine vinegar
- 6 tablespoons freshly grated Parmesan cheese
- 1 teaspoon paprika

Rosemary Glaze
- 1/2 teaspoon light olive oil

½ cup sliced shallots [about 3 medium cloves]

½ cup fresh shiitake mushrooms, cut into ¼-inch [¾-cm] slices

1 teaspoon chopped fresh rosemary

1½ cups low-sodium vegetable stock

1 tablespoon white wine vinegar

1 teaspoon arrowroot

1 teaspoon low-sodium tamari

Garnish

4 cups frozen peas

2 sprigs fresh mint

1 tablespoon sugar

⅛ teaspoon salt

To Prepare the Chickpea Custard

1. Measure the water into a large nonstick saucepan. Slowly drizzle the chickpea flour into the cold water, beating constantly with a wire whisk to keep lumps from forming. Bring to a boil over medium heat, stirring often.

2. Add the salt, pepper, saffron, and Poland Ethmix. Stir to combine. Continue cooking slowly, stirring occasionally, until the custard starts to thicken, 15 or 20 minutes. Do not allow the mixture to thicken too much; it should be the consistency of pancake batter, not polenta.

3. Remove from the heat and stir in the lemon juice and capers. Set aside.

To Prepare the Onion and Potato Layer

4. Warm the oil in a large frying pan over medium-high heat. Cook the onions and caraway seeds for about 10 minutes, or until the onions are wilted and browned. Remove a generous ¼ cup of the onions from the pan and set aside for later.

5. Reduce the heat to medium and add the potatoes to the frying pan. Season with the salt, pepper, and vinegar. Cover and cook, stirring often, for 15 minutes, or until potatoes are just tender.

6. Sprinkle 4 tablespoons of the Parmesan cheese over the top of

*Poland Ethmix

Making blends of spices and seasonings is well worth the few moments of effort it requires. Here is a recipe for the blend used in this recipe. Tucked away in a glass jar with a tight lid, it will keep all year long. You'll find interesting spices for this and other blends in natural food stores, ethnic markets, and many supermarkets. For more information about seasoning blends, see Chapter 14.

4 teaspoons caraway powder

1½ teaspoons dried marjoram

3 whole juniper berries

½ teaspoon ground cloves

½ teaspoon white pepper

Grind to a fine powder in a clean coffee mill and add 3 teaspoons of dried dill weed.

*Yellow Finn Potatoes

Potato shopping is much more fun these days with most supermarkets carrying a wide variety of spuds. Yellow Finns, grown in bumper crops in the Skagit Valley near my home, are small, oval, often irregular potatoes with a yellow skin and meat. Boasting a rich buttery flavor, they are excellent for boiling, baking, and roasting.

the potatoes, cover, and set aside.

7. Combine the $1/4$ cup of reserved onions with the remaining 2 tablespoons of Parmesan cheese and the paprika.

*To Assemble in a MEV Mold**

8. Spray the cups and lid of a MEV mold with cooking spray.

9. Divide the reserved onion mixture among six MEV cups. Spoon a layer of chickpea custard into each cup and follow with a thin layer of potatoes. Add more custard, then another thin layer of potatoes. Top with custard.

10. Rap the pan sharply on the kitchen counter two or three times to settle the mixture. Smooth the top of each cup and wipe away any excess. Cover with the oiled tray and let rest for 1 hour.

To Assemble in a Pie Dish

11. Spray a 10-inch [25-cm] quiche dish or pie plate with cooking spray.

12. Pour half of the chickpea custard into the dish. Layer the potatoes over the custard, then add the rest of the chickpea batter. Top with the reserved onion mixture. Gently press the onions down into the batter with a rubber spatula. Set aside and let rest for 1 hour.

To Bake the Tart

13. Preheat the oven to 350 degrees F [180 degrees C].

14. Bake the MEV mold for 35 minutes, the pie dish for 45 minutes. Remove from the oven and set aside for 10 minutes to allow the contents to set before serving.

To Prepare the Glaze

15. While the tart is baking, heat the oil in a large saucepan. Sauté the shallots until softened, about 2 minutes. Stir in the mushrooms and continue to sauté for another 2 minutes.

16. Add the rosemary, stock, and vinegar. Boil vigorously until reduced by half, about 15 minutes. Strain the liquid into a small saucepan, discarding the mushrooms and shallots.

17. Combine the arrowroot with 1 tablespoon of water to make a slurry. Add the slurry and the tamari to the saucepan and stir over medium heat until the mixture clears and thickens.

To Prepare the Garnish

18. While the sauce is reducing, bring ½ cup of water to a boil in a medium saucepan. Add the peas, mint, sugar, and salt. Reduce the heat and simmer for 3 to 5 minutes, or until the peas are tender but still bright green. Discard the mint sprigs.

To Serve

19. Arrange a bed of peas on each plate. Place an unmolded MEV serving or pie wedge on top of the peas. Spoon rosemary sauce over the tart. Place three broiled tomato halves alongside each serving.

Time Estimate

Hands-on, 1 hour; unsupervised, 1 hour and 45 minutes.

Nutritional Profile per Serving

340 calories; 5 g fat; 1 g saturated fat; 13% of calories from fat; 57 g carbohydrate; 13 g dietary fiber.

Broiled Tomatoes

SERVES 6

9 medium round tomatoes [not plum tomatoes]
1/8 teaspoon salt
1/8 teaspoon freshly ground black pepper

1. Preheat the broiler. Spray a broiling pan with cooking spray.

2. Cut the tomatoes in half across the girth and dry the cut surfaces gently with a paper towel. Sprinkle with salt and pepper and set on the oiled pan, cut side up.

3. Broil for 5 minutes, or until soft and lightly browned.

Time Estimate
Hands-on, 20 minutes.

Nutritional Profile per Serving
39 calories; 1 g fat; 0 g saturated fat; 14% of calories from fat; 9 g carbohydrate; 2 g dietary fiber.

Blintzes with Strawberries

I can never think of New York without thinking of blintzes—those creamy, comforting packets oozing with cheese and butter and fat. Rather than deprive myself of this quintessential New York treat, I have managed to retain the creamy texture and luxurious taste while tossing out a good number of calories. The sauce is a pleasantly piquant strawberry salsa with a surprising edge that people seem to love.

SERVES 6

*Crêpe Batter**
- 1 whole egg
- 1 egg yolk
- 1 cup skim milk
- 1/2 cup all-purpose flour
- 1 teaspoon light olive oil

Strawberry Salsa
- 3 cups chopped fresh strawberries [about 2 pints whole berries]
- 1 medium crisp apple, unpeeled, chopped [about 1 cup]
- 1 small jalapeño pepper, cored, seeded, and finely chopped
- 1 tablespoon sugar
- 1/8 teaspoon freshly ground black pepper

Crêpe Filling
- 3/4 cup yogurt cheese [page 37]
- 1/4 cup chopped dried strawberries*
- 2 teaspoons maple syrup
- 1/4 teaspoon vanilla extract
- 2 teaspoons cornstarch

1. To prepare the crêpe batter, beat the whole egg, egg yolk, and milk in a large bowl. Whisk in the flour and oil. Let the batter rest for 30 minutes before cooking.

2. While the batter is resting, prepare the salsa. In a small bowl,

*Dried Fruits:

The increasing variety of dried fruits is a real boon for low-fat cooks. Dried fruits are intensely flavored and provide textural interest to many dishes. You'll find dried fruits in the produce section of your supermarket, or perhaps near the shelf that offers raisins and prunes. Natural food stores often have a nice selection. For direct mail sales, contact:

Chukar Cherry Company, Inc.
[800] 624-9544

*Making Crêpes

The key to making good crêpes is the temperature of the pan. You'll need to experiment with your stove and your cookware, but try to reach a true medium temperature that will keep the pan at a consistent temperature.

combine the chopped strawberries, apple, and jalapeño. Sprinkle with the sugar and black pepper, and set aside.

3. To prepare the filling, gently combine the yogurt cheese, dried strawberries, maple syrup, vanilla, and cornstarch in a small bowl. Set aside while you cook the crêpes.

4. To cook the crêpes, spray a medium [7-inch or 18-cm] crêpe pan or skillet with cooking spray and warm over medium heat. It is important that the skillet be good and warm before adding the batter. Pour a scant $1/4$ cup of the batter into the pan, gently tilting the pan back and forth to coat the bottom with batter. When the top dulls and bubbles form, 30 to 45 seconds, flip the crêpe onto a paper towel, cooked side up. The crêpe will be a pale golden color on the cooked side.

5. Repeat this process with the remaining batter, spraying the skillet with cooking spray if needed to keep the crêpes from sticking. You may go ahead and fill each crêpe while the next one is cooking, or you may stack the finished crêpes until ready to fill.

6. To fill the blintzes, spoon 2 generous tablespoons of the filling into the center of the cooked side of a crêpe. Fold the edges in toward the center to make a small square envelope. Repeat with the remaining crêpes. If they will not be cooked immediately, store the blintzes seam side down in a single layer in a shallow container. They will keep in the refrigerator overnight.

7. When ready to cook the blintzes, preheat the broiler. Spray a baking sheet with cooking spray and lay the filled crêpes on the baking sheet, seam side down. Spray the tops of the blintzes with cooking spray and broil for 5 minutes, or until golden brown.

8. To serve, spread a generous $1/2$ cup of the salsa on each dessert plate. Lay a hot blintz on top of the salsa.

Time Estimate
Hands-on, 30 minutes; unsupervised, 30 minutes.

Nutritional Profile per Serving

193 calories; 3 g fat; 1 g saturated fat; 14% of calories from fat; 34 g carbohydrate; 3 g dietary fiber.

Portability

You may prepare the blintzes at home through Step 6, but wait and broil them just before serving. Carry them in a single layer inside a shallow container. The salsa can travel in a resealable bag or airtight plastic container.

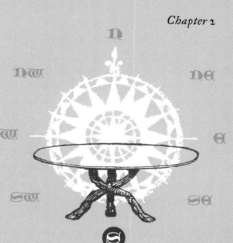

soup

Red Pepper Soup Turnberry Isle

Sweet roasted red peppers blended smooth and, floating atop, a savory toast with avocado spread.

main course

Sea Bass with Mango Chutney

Broiled fillets of sea bass with a bright fruit chutney.

vegetarian option

Broiled Artichoke Bottoms with Mango Chutney

side dish

Couscous with Peppers

Large grain Tunisian "pasta" cooked with multicolored peppers.

vegetable

Steamed Asparagus

Layered in a steamer with fresh tarragon.

dessert

Poppyseed Angel Cake with Mixed Berries

Light-as-air cake gets a slight crunch and a warm berry and wine sauce.

travelogue

*A*s we sailed south along the eastern seaboard, Treena and I began to get our "sea legs." Commodore John Burton Hall made sure we felt right at home, and we got acquainted with our fellow passengers. Early on our second morning at sea, towering palm trees on the shoreline announced we had arrived in Florida, and soon we were docking at Port Everglades. This deep harbor at the mouth of the New River hosts a constant parade of cruise ships and private yachts, and Fort Lauderdale offers a range of amenities for vacationers of different interests. Outdoor types can build sandcastles on white sandy beaches or watch for manatees in the harbor. Art and history buffs can stroll the scenic riverwalk along the banks of the New River and while away hours in the Museum

FORT LAUDERDALE
Sunshine, Citrus, and Seafood

of Art. And anyone interested in food can choose from hundreds of restaurants within walking distance or hop into a water taxi and float down a canal in search of just the right waterside café. Over three hundred miles of canals wind through Fort Lauderdale, the results of an ambitious dredging project in the early 1900s that created Port Everglades and drained the surrounding land, making it available first for agriculture and then for the million people who have made this their home.

Despite its current popularity with tourists and new residents alike, the "Venice of America" was not always considered such a desirable destination. Spanish explorers met with a less than hospitable

Early on our second morning at sea, towering palm trees announced we had arrived in Florida.

welcome from the bands of Native Americans who fished and hunted along the shore. The mouth of the New River was a shallow shoal whose shifting sands discouraged navigation, and a vast swamp extended inland in all directions. An army colonel who surveyed the area after the United States bought Florida in 1821 found two British families farming the scattered spots of high ground near the river. I was interested to learn that one of these farmers, a William Cooley, was digging local coontie roots and processing them into arrowroot starch, which he sold for cash. I am a big fan of arrowroot as a thickening agent for sauces, and I had to resist an impulse to pull on hipwaders and set off in search of some coontie roots.

I also turned down an invitation to go alligator wrestling in the Everglades in order to visit an interesting young chef named Todd Weisz. Treena and I located him several miles south of Fort Lauderdale at the Turnberry Isle Resort, an elegant Mediterranean-style retreat for folks who love to play golf and tennis, relax in the sun, hit the beach, and visit the spa. The heartbeat of the resort is the wonderful kitchen run with a light, creative touch by Chef Weisz. Todd is truly committed to the search for food that offers great taste with little risk to one's health. We spent a sunny afternoon relaxing on the hotel terrace and discussing the wonders of working as a chef in a subtropical climate with a constant supply of fresh fruits, vegetables, and seafood from which to fashion a dinner, no matter what the season.

Previous page:
I set up my camera at Turnberry Island Resort.
Fresh limes, the fruit of Florida's sunshine cuisine.

This page, from top:
Port Everglades hosts a constant cruise parade.
Getting to know Commodore John Burton Hall.
Chef Todd Weisz, Turnberry Island Resort.

The roots of this "sunshine cuisine" extend back thousands of years to native peoples who dined on a wide menu of local fish and shellfish, deer, bear, and prickly pear. Early settlers of European descent applied their own cooking techniques to these indigenous foods and planted citrus trees and other agricultural crops that greatly broadened the selection. Immigrants from Cuba and Latin America enriched the culinary culture with bright notes of color and intense flavor.

These are the traditions drawn upon in designing a light and healthy menu based upon the bounty of Florida's Gold Coast. We begin with a sunny red pepper soup, then move on to fresh sea bass topped by a spicy mango chutney. For a side dish, couscous and crisp peppers are laced with a delicate lime and arrowroot sauce in memory of Mr. William Cooley and his coontie roots. We finish with a colorful splash of berry sauce over lemon-scented poppy seed cake. The entire meal contains just over 700 calories [only 565

The roots of this "sunshine cuisine" extend back thousands of years to native peoples who dined on a wide menu of local fish and shellfish, deer, bear, and prickly pear.

calories in the vegetarian dinner]. All the dishes are low in saturated fat but high in sun-ripened flavor.

When it comes to choosing a beverage, tall glasses of iced Earl Grey tea garnished with mint and lemon are just right. For a wine, I suggest an Ariel chardonnay spiked with a thin slice of Florida's pride and joy: fresh oranges.

This page, from top:
We film a winetasting for our friends at Ariel.
Our son Andrew and a film crew join us in port.
Dining at the resort: a luxury experience.

Red Pepper Soup Turnberry Isle

One of the warm-weather vegetables of which I am especially fond is the red bell pepper, featured here in a robust-flavored soup reminiscent of a creation I enjoyed at Turnberry Isle Resort. In addition to its cuisine, the resort at Turnberry Isle is famous for the Island Green on its golf course—a green almost completely surrounded by water. As a salute to this water trap, I created a Floating Avocado Toast [page 37] to sail atop the rich red pepper soup. The toast's crispness contrasts nicely with the rounded sweetness of the soup—a satisfying start to this coastal dinner.

SERVES 6

- 4 large red bell peppers
- 4 fresh Italian plum tomatoes, such as Roma
- 1/2 teaspoon light olive oil
- 1/2 cup finely diced onion
- 2 cloves garlic, peeled, bashed, and minced
- 4 cups low-sodium chicken stock
- 1/8 teaspoon salt
- 1/8 teaspoon freshly ground black pepper
- 1 teaspoon balsamic vinegar
- 6 fresh basil stems

1. Preheat the broiler.

2. Cut both ends off the peppers and remove the seeds and pulp. Slice each pepper twice from top to bottom to make three rectangular sections. Press the pieces flat with the palm of your hand. Remove the stems from the caps and press the caps flat.

3. Place the pepper pieces, skin side up, on a broiler pan and broil until the skins blacken and blister.

4. Transfer the peppers to a paper or plastic bag, seal the bag, and set aside for at least 10 minutes to steam. When the peppers are cool enough to handle, peel and discard the charred skins. Chop the remaining flesh and set aside.

5. Bring a large saucepan of water to a rolling boil. Drop the

tomatoes into the boiling water for 1 minute. [This will loosen the skin enough to peel.] Transfer the tomatoes to a basin of cold water or allow them to cool on a plate. When the tomatoes are cool enough to handle, peel and discard the loose skins.

6. Quarter each tomato lengthwise and scoop the seeds into a strainer set over a bowl. Discard the seeds and reserve the juice. Dice the tomatoes and set aside.

7. Warm the oil in a large saucepan over medium heat. Sauté the onion until soft but not browned, about 2 minutes. Add the garlic and cook an additional 3 minutes. Stir in the peppers, tomatoes, reserved tomato juice, stock, salt, pepper, and vinegar. [Vegetarian Option: Use vegetable stock here.] Bruise the basil stems and tie them in a bundle with string, or enclose in a mesh herb ball. Drop the stems into the stock, cover, and bring to a boil. Reduce the heat and simmer for 10 minutes. Remove the basil stems.

8. Transfer half of the soup to a blender or food processor and purée until smooth. Return the purée to the pan and stir well. Reheat the soup before serving.

Vegetarian Option
Use vegetable stock in Step 7.

Floating Avocado Toast
[*Garlic Toast with Avocado Yogurt Cheese Spread*]
> 6   slices [1/2-inch thick] of French baguette
> 1   whole clove garlic, peeled [optional]
> 1   ripe avocado
> 1/4   cup yogurt cheese*
> 1/8   teaspoon salt
> 1   teaspoon fresh lime juice

Garnish
> 6   fresh basil leaves

*Yogurt Cheese

Substituting strained yogurt for butter, mayonnaise, or other high-fat spreads could reduce your fat consumption by 47,000 calories per year. It just takes a few moments of hands-on time to make. I spread it on toast in the morning with a bit of marmalade and often use it to make creamy sauces for pasta, vegetables, fish or chicken. If you like the taste of yogurt, you'll like the slight tartness of its concentrated form. Some people prefer to smooth the taste with a touch of soy milk. Whichever way you prefer, here are the simple directions:

> 1 1/2   cups [354 ml] plain nonfat
>   yogurt, no gelatin added

Put the yogurt in a strainer over a bowl [*see Tools, page 224*]. Or you can use a coffee filter, piece of muslin, or a paper towel and place it in a small sieve over a bowl. Cover and let it drain in the refrigerator for 12 hours or overnight. It becomes quite firm and the small lumps disappear, which makes it ideal for use in sauces. The liquid whey drains into the bowl, leaving you with thick, creamy yogurt cheese.

1. Preheat the broiler.

2. Place the bread slices on a broiler pan and toast until lightly browned on both sides. Remove from the oven and rub one side of each slice with the garlic.

3. To prepare the spread, peel and pit the avocado. Mash the avocado with a fork until it has the consistency of chunky guacamole. Stir in the yogurt cheese, salt, and lime juice. If you will not be serving this immediately, lay a piece of plastic wrap directly on the surface of the spread so it won't darken, then cover with an airtight lid and refrigerate until needed.

4. To serve, slice the basil leaves into thin slivers. Spread the avocado mixture thickly on the garlic toast. Spoon the hot soup into warmed bowls, float an "avocado island" in the center of each bowl, and sprinkle with basil.

Time Estimate
Hands-on, 25 minutes.

Nutritional Profile per Serving
126 calories; 4 g fat; 1 g saturated fat; 26% of calories from fat; 20 g carbohydrate; 2 g dietary fiber.

Portability
Pour cooled soup into a plastic container with a tight-fitting lid. Toast the bread, rub with garlic, and transport in a flat airtight container. The spread will be at its very best if you wait and make it at the party. If you must make it ahead, transport it in the same container in which it was refrigerated.

Sea Bass with Mango Chutney

This entrée is a sparkling example of Todd Weisz' ability to bring bright notes of flavor to healthy dishes. I've changed his black grouper to sea bass because I think it will be easier for you to find in the market. If you don't see it fresh, order some—sea bass has a meaty texture that is hard to duplicate. Also, I think you will love the rich taste, which is surprising considering its low-fat qualities! Serve this dish with Mango Chutney [page 41] and Couscous with Peppers [page 42]. Fresh Steamed Asparagus [page 44] puts the finishing touch on a beautiful plate. Do remember to make the chutney and start the couscous before you cook the fish!

SERVES 6

1/4	teaspoon salt
1/4	teaspoon freshly ground black pepper
1 1/2	tablespoons finely chopped fresh tarragon
1 1/2	tablespoons finely chopped fresh parsley
1 1/2	tablespoons finely chopped fresh chives
1 1/2	tablespoons finely chopped fresh basil
6	sea bass fillets, about 6 ounces [168 g] each

Vegetarian Option [per Serving]
2 artichoke bottoms

1. Preheat the broiler.

2. Sprinkle the salt and pepper on a large plate, then spray the plate with cooking spray. Mix the tarragon, parsley, chives, and basil in a small bowl and sprinkle a third of this mixture over the plate.

3. Drag the fish fillets one at a time across the plate to pick up the seasonings, then place on a broiler pan, herbed side down. Sprinkle the fillets with another third of the herb mixture, then spray the tops of the fish lightly with cooking spray. [Save the rest of the herbs for garnish.]

4. Broil the fillets for 4 minutes on each side, or until the flesh is no longer translucent, but white throughout.

*Chilean Sea Bass

Moist, tender, and white, this fish has a wonderful "mouthfeel" but very little fat. People who are reducing the amount of red meat in their diets often find sea bass very satisfying. Also called Patagonian Tooth Fish, these sea monsters weigh in at thirty to sixty pounds and live in the deep subtropical waters of South America and Africa. Sea bass freezes very well, and you can almost always find it frozen in your supermarket if it is not available fresh.

Mangoes

To choose a mango, look for one that gives slightly to soft pressure from the palm of your hand. California "Keitt" mangoes are ripe when their skin is dark green and the flesh is soft; the more common mangoes have orange skins. Mangoes have a long flat pit that lays horizontally through the middle of the fruit and can be difficult to remove. The best method I have found is to lay the palm of your hand over the mango, steadying the fruit horizontally against the table. To loosen the fruit from the pit, angle the knife blade up over the top of the pit, using a sawing motion and just touching the pit itself with the knife blade. When one side is loosened, turn the mango over and make another cut, using the same sawing motion. This will leave you with two halves and a pit. Trim any remaining flesh from the pit. Cut each half into four wedges and peel each wedge, running a thin knife blade between the flesh and the peel. Cut the wedges into $1/2$-inch pieces.

5. Serve the fish on top of a bed of couscous. Heap a spoonful of mango chutney on top of each fillet and sprinkle the reserved herb mixture over all.

Time Estimate
Hands-on, 20 minutes; unsupervised, 8 minutes.

Nutritional Profile per Serving
197 calories; 4 g fat; 1 g saturated fat; 16% of calories from fat; 8 g carbohydrate; 1 g dietary fiber.

Vegetarian Option: Broiled Artichoke Bottoms
Substitute 2 artichoke bottoms for each serving of fish. Season the artichoke bottoms with the mixed herbs and broil just until heated through and slightly browned, about 4 minutes. Serve over couscous, as you would the fish, and top with the chutney. Garnish with the chopped herbs.

Vegetarian Option Nutritional Profile per Serving
45 calories; 0 g fat; 0 g saturated fat; 3% of calories from fat; 10 g carbohydrate; 0 g dietary fiber.

Mango Chutney

Although native to India and southeast Asia, mango trees seem quite at home in southern Florida, where their luxurious green leaves shade many lucky backyards. The fruit is wonderfully sweet, and some people believe it has a natural cooling effect as well.

  1   fresh mango,* peeled, pitted, and chopped [1 cup]
2-3   green onions, white parts only,
        cut into 1/4-inch [3/4-cm] slices [1/2 cup]
  1   tablespoon peeled, grated fresh gingerroot
1/2   cup fruity white wine
        [I prefer dealcoholized blanc]
1/4   teaspoon angostura bitters*
1/4   teaspoon minced habañero chile,* cored and
        seeded, or 1/4 teaspoon cayenne pepper

Combine the mango, onion, ginger, wine, bitters, and chile in a small saucepan. Bring to a boil over medium heat, then reduce the heat and simmer for 10 minutes. Remove from the heat and set aside until ready to serve. This chutney will keep for a day or so in the refrigerator.

*Angostura Bitters

Used in small amounts, angostura bitters lend an aromatic and slightly bitter element to mixed drinks. Made in Trinidad from roots, bark, leaves and alcohol, these bitters can be found in the beverage department of your supermarket. I've used it here to add a touch of sharpness to my Mango Chutney.

*Habañero Chiles

Have you heard of Mr. Scoville? He must be the man behind Scoville heat units, and I think of him every time I eat a bit of habañero chile. Measured on this international scale of hotness, the habañero is the hottest of all chilies—1,000 times hotter than a jalapeño! Habañeros are bright yellow-orange, shaped like lanterns, and should be handled only while wearing plastic gloves. Similar to Scotch Bonnets, they may be found in your supermarket or a good Latin American grocery.

Couscous with Peppers

Couscous, made from tiny bits of semolina coated with wheat flour, is a staple food in a number of cultures, particularly North Africa. Its feathery texture makes a wonderful accompaniment to fish, and I've dressed up its pale color with some bright peppers and red onion for this festive dish. Your friends will have time to assemble their dishes while the couscous is cooking, and you'll have time to finish preparing the main course.

SERVES 6

3	cups low-sodium chicken or vegetable stock*
1/4	teaspoon almond extract
1	cup large-grain couscous*
3	tablespoons finely diced red bell pepper
3	tablespoons finely diced yellow bell pepper
3	tablespoons finely diced red onion
2	tablespoons lime juice [1 lime]
1/2	teaspoon finely chopped cilantro stems
1	teaspoon arrowroot
2	teaspoons water
1/8	teaspoon salt
1	tablespoon finely sliced cilantro leaves
1/2	cup fruity white wine [I prefer dealcoholized blanc]

1. Combine the stock and almond extract in a large saucepan and bring to a boil. Toss in any vegetable or fish trimmings left over from preparing the main course. [Vegetarian Option: Use vegetable stock and do not add fish trimmings.] Simmer for 10 minutes or so. Strain, discard the trimmings, and return the stock to the saucepan.

2. Stir the couscous into the stock and simmer for 20 minutes or until fluffy and dry. If the couscous is too runny, drain the excess liquid. If the couscous is too dry, add up to 1/2 cup of water or dealcoholized wine. [If you only have alcoholic wine available, boil off the alcohol before adding it to the couscous or the dish will be bitter.]

•Chicken Stock

The stock for this recipe can be made richer by adding the fish bones and vegetable trimmings to the chicken stock, then simmering it over low heat while you prepare the rest of the meal.

•Couscous

Large-grain couscous has grains about the size of peppercorns, while regular couscous is very similar to Cream of Wheat in size. I use Middle Eastern-style couscous from Pitter's Pantry. If you're unable to find it, call the Specialty Foods Manager at Larry's Markets in Bellevue, Washington at [206] 453-0600.

You can use regular-grain couscous in place of the large-grain couscous with just a few changes. It will result in a very different dish and I do encourage you to look for the larger grain Middle Eastern-style for an unusual treat. If you choose regular-grain couscous, reduce the stock to 2 cups and the wine at the end to 1/4 cup. Bring the stock to a boil, add the couscous, cover and let rest off the heat for 5 minutes. Stir in the slurry and then the other ingredients and serve while it is still hot.

3. While the couscous is cooking, combine the peppers and onion in a small bowl. Add the lime juice and cilantro stems and mix.

4. In another small bowl, mix the arrowroot with 2 teaspoons of water to make a slurry.

5. As soon as the couscous is done, stir in the slurry. [It is important to add the slurry while the couscous is still very hot.] Add the pepper mixture and the salt, then remove the pan from the heat and cover tightly to keep warm.

6. When ready to serve, stir the cilantro leaves and wine into the couscous.

Time Estimate
Hands-on, 20 minutes; unsupervised, 20 minutes.

Nutritional Profile per Serving
144 calories; 2 g fat; 1 g saturated fat; 12% of calories from fat; 26 g carbohydrate; 2 g dietary fiber.

Vegetarian Option
Cook the couscous in vegetable stock instead of chicken stock and do not add fish trimmings to the stock in Step 1.

Steamed Asparagus

This method produces perfectly cooked asparagus—the stems and tips cook evenly when they are arranged carefully in a steamer. The small bit of extra effort is well worth it when this beautiful vegetable is cast as a star performer.

Serves 6

  2   pounds [900 g] fresh asparagus, trimmed
  1/8 teaspoon salt
  1/4 teaspoon freshly ground black pepper
  1   sprig of fresh tarragon
  1   lemon, juiced [about 2 tablespoons]

1. Partially fill a saucepan or steamer pot with water and bring to a boil. Double a piece of waxed paper and arrange it so that it covers half the openings in your steamer basket or platform. Place the heads of the asparagus spears over the waxed paper and the stems over the open holes. [This allows the thick stems to get more steam and cook more quickly than the tender spears.]

2. Sprinkle the asparagus with the salt and pepper, then lay the sprig of tarragon over the top.

3. Place the steamer over the boiling water, cover, and steam for 8 minutes, or until crisp-tender. The thickness of the asparagus will dictate the time necessary to cook it.

4. Remove from the heat, sprinkle with the lemon juice, and serve immediately.

Time Estimate
Hands-on, 10 minutes; unsupervised, 8 minutes.

Nutritional Profile per Serving
52 calories; 1 g fat; 0 g saturated fat; 14% of calories from fat; 9 g carbohydrate; 4 g dietary fiber.

Poppy Seed Angel Cake with Mixed Berries

In our search to eliminate excess fat from our diets but still enjoy the foods we love, I continue to be impressed by Susan Purdy and her baking books: "Have Your Cake and Eat It, Too" and "Let Them Eat Cake." I've adopted several of her techniques in this simple cake recipe. The poppy seeds introduce an unusual texture, and the berry sauce adds a sweet-tart touch of flavor that I find quite enticing.

SERVES 6

2	cups sifted cake flour
1/2	cup sifted confectioners' sugar
1/2	teaspoon salt
3/4	cup superfine sugar*
1 1/2	cups egg whites [10 to 12 large eggs], at room temperature
1	teaspoon cream of tartar
1	teaspoon vanilla extract
1	teaspoon grated lemon zest
2	teaspoons poppy seeds

Berry Sauce

1	pound [450 g] fresh or frozen mixed berries
1	cup fruity white wine [I prefer dealcoholized blanc]
1	tablespoon cornstarch
1	tablespoon sugar

Garnish

Edible flowers*
Mint sprigs

To Prepare the Cake

1. Preheat the oven to 325 degrees F [165 degrees C]. Make sure the egg whites are at room temperature before you begin the recipe.

2. Resift the cake flour with the confectioners' sugar and salt onto a piece of waxed paper.

3. Sift the superfine sugar onto a separate sheet of waxed paper.

*Superfine Sugar

To make superfine sugar, simply spin granulated sugar in your blender for a few minutes. This makes the granules smaller and gives better texture to cakes and meringues.

*Edible Flowers

Small edible flowers can add dazzling color to simple dishes, but be sure that they are completely chemical-free. Use violets, garlic, chive, and other herb blossoms or tiny nasturtiums as a highlight for salads or a garnish on desserts. For a special occasion, "candy" small blossoms by brushing them lightly with egg white, dipping them in superfine sugar, and placing in an oven at 200 degrees for about an hour. This is a task that children love because it produces such spectacular results.

4. Make sure the bowl and whip attachment of your electric mixer are perfectly clean and grease-free. Beat the egg whites and cream of tartar on medium speed until foamy, about 1 minute. Beat on high speed for an additional 3 minutes, or until the whites are very glossy and moist, with soft peaks. Begin adding the superfine sugar, 1 tablespoon at a time, and continue beating until the whites form stiff peaks, but are not dry. Add the vanilla and lemon zest and mix just long enough to incorporate. The egg whites should not move or slide when you turn the bowl upside down. [Careful!]

5. Sprinkle the flour mixture over the beaten egg whites, 3 tablespoons at a time, folding gently with a rubber spatula after each addition. Fold in the poppy seeds.

6. Spoon the batter into an *ungreased* angel food cake pan or tube pan with a removable bottom. Bake for 45 minutes, or until a cake tester inserted in the center of the cake comes out clean. Remove from the oven and, without disturbing the cake, turn the pan upside down onto its legs, or fit the tube over the neck of a bottle. Let the cake cool completely in its upside-down position so that it won't collapse.

7. When the cake is completely cool, take it down from its perch and run a thin knife blade around the edge of the pan and the central tube to loosen. The cake will stay fresh for several days if wrapped in plastic wrap and stored at room temperature.

8. When ready to serve, slice into wedges using a serrated knife so that you don't compress the airy center.

To Prepare the Sauce

9. Mix half of the berries with the wine in a medium saucepan and cook over medium heat until the fruit has softened. Press the mixture through a sieve set over a second medium saucepan, and discard the pulp.

10. Combine the cornstarch with 2 tablespoons of water to make a slurry. Add the slurry and the sugar to the berry juice in the

saucepan. Stir over medium heat until the sugar dissolves and the sauce thickens. Add the remaining berries to the sauce and stir gently to combine.

To Serve

11. Spoon the warm berry sauce over wedges of cold angel food cake. An edible flower and a sprig of mint give the dessert a touch of elegance.

Time Estimate

Hands-on, 20 minutes; unsupervised, 45 minutes.

Nutritional Profile per Serving

199 calories; 0 g fat; 0 g saturated fat; 1% of calories from fat; 44 g carbohydrate; 3 g dietary fiber.

Portability

The cake can be made ahead and carried in a rigid plastic storage container. You'll only need half the cake for this dinner, so wrap the other half well and freeze for up to two weeks. The sauce can also be made ahead and rewarmed slightly just before serving.

salad
Spiced Spinach and Shrimp
A warm, wilted salad spiced with hot peppers and topped with shrimp.

main course
Lamb Shanks Frenchie
Juicy shanks of lamb share a wine-red sauce with steamed kale and sweet potatoes.

vegetarian option
Red Kidney Beans Frenchie

dessert
Fungi Foster
Cornmeal pudding seasoned with brown sugar and drizzled with a caramel crunch.

travelogue

There is always something exciting about approaching an island by sea, and I made sure I was on deck early for our arrival in the Virgin Islands. From a distance the scattered islands and cays appear wild and pristine, unchanged from the days when native islanders fished for turtles and tended crops of maize and sweet potatoes. Columbus sailed into these waters in 1493 and christened this cluster of islands Las Virgines in honor of Saint Ursula and her eleven thousand maiden martyrs. Columbus claimed the Virgins and the rest of the West Indies for Spain, setting off an international tug-of-war for control of the region. No one country ever gained ascendancy, and different islands fell under the control of different flags, resulting in a diverse mixture of languages and traditions.

We rounded the tip of St. Thomas and dropped anchor just beyond the picturesque harbor. Shimmering beaches fringed the turquoise waters, and small sailboats dotted the circular bay. Red-roofed houses climbed the green hillsides, giving the island an Old World look. Although St. Thomas has been owned by the United States since 1917, traces of its European legacy are still very much in evidence.

St. Thomas
A Savory Stew of Culture and Cuisine

Previous page:
Visiting the market in St. Thomas.

The market's matriarch: Sanderilla Indiana Blyden Thomas, known as "Mrs. Sandy".

This page, from top:
The scattered islands and pristine cays of the Virgin islands.

Gail Shulterbrandt-Rivera, L.D., a gracious and knowledgeable hostess.

Talented young island Chef Jason Budsan.

In the two hundred years after Columbus, St. Thomas passed through Spanish, Dutch, British, and French hands before being purchased by Denmark in 1672. The Danes planted sugarcane, indigo, and cotton on the steep hillsides and imported slaves from Africa to work the fields. Within a few years the port of Charlotte Amalie had grown into an international trading center. Its natural deepwater harbor provided safe moorage for a steady stream of

Shimmering beaches fringed turquoise waters, and small sailboats dotted the bay.

European traders and African slave ships, and Danish officials gave a cordial welcome to the fast sloops of pirates such a Blackbeard. We were more interested in organic farming than pirates—more squashbuckling than swashbuckling, you might say—and set off to find the "foods of the people." We were accorded a warm Caribbean greeting by Mrs. Gail Shulterbrandt-Rivera, L.D., who graciously invited us to enjoy some wonderful local foods at her home. Gail is the director of Special Nutrition Programs for the Virgin Islands Department of Education, and we had a great deal of fun talking about ways to introduce mainland cooks to the ingredients and seasonings that are unique to the islands. Caribbean cuisine has a most colorful history, reflecting a mixture of cooking traditions from many different cultures, and it is fascinating to trace the evolution of certain dishes and their variations from island to island.

One of the most interesting examples of this culinary melting pot is callaloo, a dish that appears in myriad variations [and spellings] on different islands. Sometimes a smooth soup, sometimes a hearty stew, it is based on callaloo, the tender young leaves of certain native plants. It usually contains okra, salt pork [some recipes call for a pickled pig's tail], and often crab or shrimp as well. Food historians believe that callaloo originated in slave kitchens as a sort of opportunistic stew combining available meat or shellfish with native greens from the woods and okra from kitchen gardens. The stew was simmered in a cast-iron pot hung over the kitchen fire and seasoned with herbs and hot peppers. The version of callaloo which we sampled was delicious and supremely nourishing and was accompanied by a fireworks display of very hot pepper sauce, a condiment that dates back to pre-Columbian times. The natives that Columbus visited called their spice *aji*, and he noted that "the people won't eat without it, for they find it very wholesome." Today's islanders agree, and locally brewed pepper sauce of multiple hues and fieriness is a common cottage industry throughout the Caribbean.

During our visit to St. Thomas, we were also fortunate to meet Jacquel Dawson, a talented entrepreneur and founder of Project Bush Tea, which employs local women to process and package over a dozen varieties of aromatic teas. For generations, local people have harvested leaves from more than four hundred native plants and brewed medicinal teas to treat ailments such as fever, headaches, and upset stomachs. The varieties we sampled ranged from delicate concoctions to smoky, robust brews, and we found them to be both healthful in their effect and headily delicious, either hot or cold.

Another new friend we met in Charlotte Amalie was Chef Jason Budsan, a young islander descended from a group of French fishermen and farmers who settled on the island in the 1800s. A graduate of Johnson and Wales University College of Culinary Arts, Jason is a wealth of practical information and is presently developing a commercial line of vinegars and oils infused with local herbs and spices.

As we sailed away from this little island paradise, I thought about the true tastes of this cuisine layered by generations of the cooking of many cultures. This "melting pot" dinner includes a "cousin-once-removed" to the hearty callaloo, using spinach instead of callaloo greens and shrimp rather than pickled pig's tail. Fresh

The tastes of this cuisine were layered by many generations and cultures.

chile sauce adds zing and reminds us of Columbus's first taste of hot peppers. The main dish of lamb shanks reflects the continuing French influence on the island. I combine it here with steamed kale and native sweet potatoes, which hearken back to the crops of pre-Columbian islanders. You can adapt the spiciness to the tastes of your guests by serving a hot pepper sauce on the side. The rustic dessert soufflé is derived from the cornmeal mush that was a staple of the island's West African slaves.

This entire rich and hearty meal easily fits within our 1000-calorie framework—if you choose the lamb shanks, the menu totals 632 calories and 11 grams of fat. The vegetarian option offers similar robust flavors with 651 calories and 7 fat grams.

This page, from top:
We tour an outstanding organic farm with one of the owners.

Acting up with good friend John Foster [*below*].

Spiced Spinach and Shrimp

This appetizer takes its inspiration from the wonderful flavors of the famous Caribbean callaloo. Spicy fresh shrimp top a bed of sautéed spinach, and a tropical hint of lemongrass sets the stage for an island evening with friends.

SERVES 6

1	stalk fresh lemongrass° about 3 inches [8 cm]
1	teaspoon finely chopped fresh thyme
1/4	teaspoon salt
1/4	teaspoon freshly ground black pepper
2	cloves garlic, peeled, bashed, and chopped
1 1/2	teaspoons light olive oil
12	medium shrimp [about 8 ounces or 225 g], peeled and rinsed
3	serrano chiles,° cored, seeded, and finely diced
3	thin slices [2 ounces or 56 g total] Canadian bacon, very finely diced
1/4	teaspoon ground nutmeg
1	bunch green onions, sliced into 1/4-inch [3/4-cm] rounds, white parts separated from green parts [1/2 cup whites and 1 cup greens]
3	bunches spinach, carefully washed, stems removed [12 cups]
1	tablespoon roughly chopped fresh parsley
1	teaspoon arrowroot
2	teaspoons balsamic vinegar

Spicy Garnish

1	serrano chile, cored, seeded, and finely chopped
1	tablespoon roughly chopped fresh parsley
	Balsamic vinegar

Vegetarian Option [per Serving]

1	red bell pepper, roasted

To Prepare the Shrimp

1. Remove the tough outside layer of the lemongrass and cut off

°Lemongrass

Lemongrass is a wonderfully versatile herb that adds a subtle fruity perfume to a variety of foods. Happily, it is becoming much more available in American supermarkets and I urge you to ask your produce manager to carry it if you are unable to find it. Used in many Thai and Vietnamese dishes, it is sold in long stalks with a bulb on one end. Peel the dry outer layers and cut the bulb into thin slices for dishes in which it will be eaten. Use the outer stalk, cut into 2 inch pieces, to flavor stocks and sauces; remove the lemongrass pieces before serving. Dried lemongrass is used for herbal teas, but I do not recommend it for flavoring food. If you are unable to find fresh lemongrass, substitute grated lemon zest.

the root end and the dry top. Slice from the root end and use only the tender bulb. Slice thinly so that the flavor can spread through the dish.

2. In a small bowl, combine the lemongrass, thyme, salt, pepper, and half of the chopped garlic.

3. Warm 1 teaspoon of the oil in a high-sided skillet over high heat. Add the shrimp and one-third of the garlic-herb mixture. Toss just until the shrimp begin to turn pink, about 1 minute. Add 1 teaspoon of the diced chiles and cook 30 seconds more. Transfer the contents of the skillet to a warmed plate, cover with a lid, and set aside. The shrimp will finish cooking from the retained heat under the lid.

To Prepare the Spinach

4. Return the skillet to the stove without washing it and add the remaining 1/2 teaspoon of oil. Cook the Canadian bacon, 1/8 teaspoon of the nutmeg, and the remaining garlic-herb mixture for 1 minute, stirring constantly. Stir in the rest of the diced chiles and the sliced onion whites. [Vegetarian Option: Omit the Canadian bacon from this step.]

5. Add one-third [about 4 cups] of the spinach to the skillet and toss the ingredients with two spoons to coat the spinach with oil and seasonings. Cover* and cook for 60 seconds. Add half the remaining spinach, again tossing to coat with oil, then cover tightly and cook for 60 seconds. Repeat with the last batch of spinach. The skillet will be full to begin with but will cook down after each addition. When all the spinach has finished cooking, the leaves will no longer be crisp but will remain bright green.

6. Scatter the green parts of the onions over the top of the spinach and sprinkle with the remaining 1/8 teaspoon of nutmeg. Cover and warm through. Stir in the parsley and remove from the heat.

7. Transfer the spinach to a strainer set over a bowl. Press as much liquid as possible out of the spinach and return the

*Serrano Chiles

These small dark green or red peppers look like small jalapeños and are second only to habañeros in heat. If you include the seeds from the chiles, the dish will be very hot; without seeds, it will be somewhat milder. Serranos are available fresh or canned at most grocery stores.

*Etoufée

A French word that means "smothered," this classic technique is used to express volatile oils and steam food in a covered pan. Food is browned, then surrounded by aromatic ingredients and simmered in a small amount of flavorful liquid. When used with fresh herbs and vegetables, this method can produce an explosion of satisfying fragrance and aroma with the use of very little fat. In this shrimp and spinach dish, chop the Canadian bacon quite finely to produce the best results.

liquid to the skillet. Keep spinach warm.

8. Combine the arrowroot and balsamic vinegar to make a slurry. Add the slurry to the spinach liquid in the skillet and stir over medium heat until the mixture is slightly thickened. Add the shrimp and cook until heated through.

To Serve

9. Arrange small mounds of spinach on individual salad plates. Set two shrimp in the center of each spinach mound and spoon a little of the thickened sauce over the shrimp.

10. To garnish, sprinkle the chopped chile and parsley over the spinach and around the rim of the plate. Pass a cruet of balsamic vinegar for the greens.

Time Estimate
Hands-on, 30 minutes.

Nutritional Profile per Serving
78 calories; 2 g fat; 0 g saturated fat; 21% of calories from fat; 6 g carbohydrate; 4 g dietary fiber.

Vegetarian Option
Leave out the shrimp [Step 3] and Canadian bacon [Step 4] and lay two shrimp-sized strips of roasted red bell pepper over the top of the spinach.

Vegetarian Option Nutritional Profile per Serving
52 calories; 2 g fat; 0 g saturated fat; 35% of calories from fat; 7 g carbohydrate; 4 g dietary fiber.

Portability
I suggest that you prepare all the ingredients as shown in the recipe list and do the cooking at the party. Pack the ingredients in small resealable bags.

Lamb Shanks Frenchie

Back in the 1800s, a group of French Huguenots arrived on St. Thomas in search of a home. Some of these refugees settled on the island's rugged northern coast, where they began carving farms from the steep, rocky hillsides. Taking advantage of the extra rainfall delivered by storms off the Atlantic, they were soon sending mules loaded with fresh produce to markets in town. Today, the north side of the island is still dotted with small farms tended by "Frenchies," as they call themselves. In honor of their contribution to the culture of the island, I have blended the red wine and herbs of Provence with some Caribbean hot peppers to give these succulent lamb shanks a special twist. Sweet potatoes and kale complete the definition of this island dish.

Serves 6

*Lamb Shanks

Shanks from lambs raised in the U.S. tend to be quite large. Ask your butcher for small New Zealand or Australian lamb shanks, which provide a more moderate serving size.

- 3 lamb shanks,* about 1 pound [450 g] each
- 1/2 teaspoon salt
- 1/4 teaspoon freshly ground black pepper
- 3-6 medium sweet potatoes [1 per person for heartier appetites]
- 1 teaspoon light olive oil
- 1 large onion, roughly diced [2 1/2 cups]
- 2 large red bell peppers, cut into 1/2-inch [1 1/2-cm] pieces [3 cups]
- 3 large cloves garlic, peeled, bashed, and chopped [1 tablespoon]
- 2 teaspoons dried thyme
- 1/8 teaspoon ground cloves
- 1/2 cup tomato paste
- 3 stalks celery, cut into 1/2-inch [1 1/2-cm] slices [1 1/2 cups]
- 1/2 teaspoon dried crushed red pepper flakes
- 2 cups dry red wine [I prefer dealcoholized Ariel Cabernet Sauvignon]
- 2 teaspoons arrowroot
- 1 tablespoon water
- 2 bunches fresh kale, washed, stemmed, and torn into bite-sized pieces [about 8 cups]

*Spurtles

I love these flat bamboo cooking utensils. They're specially shaped to reach into the corners of pots and pans, bringing up every bit of tasty goodness. You can find them in any good gourmet store, kitchen supply store, or my catalog.

Garnish

    2 tablespoons chopped fresh chives

Vegetarian Option [per Serving]

    3/4 cup cooked red kidney beans, rinsed and drained

    1/4 cup dry red wine

    1/2 teaspoon arrowroot

    1 teaspoon water

1. Preheat the oven to 350 degrees F [180 degrees C]. Position one oven rack just above the middle and another just below.

2. Pour 1/2 cup of warm water into the bottom of a roasting pan. Set the lamb shanks on a rack in the pan and sprinkle with 1/4 teaspoon of the salt and 1/8 teaspoon of the pepper. Place on the top oven rack.

3. Scrub the sweet potatoes and pierce several times with a fork. Line a baking sheet with aluminum foil, lay the sweet potatoes on the foil, and place on the bottom oven rack. [Be advised that the sweet potatoes will ooze a bit while baking. The aluminum foil will make it easier to clean the sugary syrup off the baking sheet.]

4. Remove the sweet potatoes after 45 minutes and set aside. Leave the lamb in for an additional 15 minutes, or until tender. Small lamb shanks will be tender in 1 hour, while larger ones may take up to 30 minutes longer.

5. While the lamb shanks are roasting, begin preparing the stew. Warm the oil in a large skillet over medium-high heat. Add the diced onion and peppers, toss well, and cook for 1 1/2 minutes. Sprinkle with the garlic, thyme, and cloves, and cook for another 1 1/2 minutes without stirring.

6. Add the tomato paste and toss the ingredients with spurtles* or wooden spoons, using a motion similar to tossing a salad. Continue cooking over medium-high heat until the tomato paste begins to darken and caramelize. Stir in the celery, pepper flakes, and the remaining 1/4 teaspoon of salt and 1/8 teaspoon of pepper, using the same tossing motion. Add

the wine, cover, and simmer for 30 minutes while the lamb finishes roasting. [Vegetarian Option: Set aside ¾ cup of this mixture per vegetarian serving before proceeding with the next step.]

7. Remove the lamb shanks from the oven. Cut the cooked meat from the bones using a small sharp knife and fork, discarding the obvious fat and leaving the meat in good-sized pieces, about ¾ inch [2 cm]. You should end up with about 18 ounces [500 g] of lean meat.

8. Pour 1 cup of water into the roasting pan. Scrape up the flavorful, browned bits of meat from the bottom with a spurtle or wooden spoon and stir well. Pour the liquid into a fat strainer [page 210] and let it sit for a few minutes to allow the fat to rise to the top. Pour off the strained liquid, stopping when you reach the fat. If you do not have a fat strainer, allow the liquid to cool for a few minutes and skim the fat off the top. You should end up with about ⅔ cup of fat-free liquid.

9. Mix the arrowroot with 1 tablespoon of water to form a slurry. Add the strained liquid and the reserved chunks of lamb to the vegetable mixture in the skillet. Draw the pan away from the heat, stir in the slurry, and return to the burner. Cook over medium heat, stirring often, until the sauce is slightly thickened and glossy. Remove from the heat, cover, and keep warm.

10. Place the kale in a vegetable steamer, cover, and steam for 6 minutes.

11. While the kale is cooking, finish preparing the sweet potatoes. Make a vertical cut through the skin down the length of the potato, and peel the skin away. Slice the potatoes lengthwise into quarters.

To Serve

12. Divide the kale into six portions and arrange one serving on each warmed dinner plate. Sprinkle with salt and pepper. Lay two to four sweet potato quarters down the center of the kale,

depending on appetites. Top with 1 cup of the stew and garnish with chopped chives.

Time Estimate
Hands-on, 45 minutes; unsupervised, 1 hour.

Nutritional Profile per Serving
345 calories; 7 g fat; 2 g saturated fat; 19% of calories from fat; 40 g carbohydrate; 7 g dietary fiber.

Vegetarian Option: Red Kidney Beans Frenchie
Pour the reserved 3/4 cup of the vegetable and wine sauce into a small saucepan and add the red kidney beans and wine. Heat over medium heat. Mix the arrowroot with 1 teaspoon wine or water to make a slurry. Remove the saucepan from the heat and stir in the slurry. Return the saucepan to the heat and stir until glossy and slightly thickened. Follow directions for serving.

Vegetarian Option Nutritional Profile per Serving
390 calories; 3 g fat; 0 g saturated fat; 7% of calories from fat; 75 g carbohydrate; 19 g dietary fiber.

Fungi Foster
Cornmeal Pudding with Caramel Crunch

If you appreciate Italian foods, you might think fungi was some sort of mushroom dessert. In the Caribbean, fungi refers to a versatile cornmeal mush [also called coo-coo] that is sometimes mixed with vegetables and served as a side dish and sometimes sweetened and served as dessert. I lightened the texture to create something more like a soufflé and criss-crossed the top with crunchy strands of caramelized sugar. My version of this pudding is dedicated to John and Claire Foster, dear friends and longtime residents of St. Thomas. John is an Olympic yachtsman and frequent Caribbean champion.

SERVES 6

3/4	cup evaporated skim milk
1 1/4	cups 2% milk
1	cinnamon stick, about 2 1/2 inches [6 1/2 cm] long
6	tablespoons yellow cornmeal
2	teaspoons cornstarch
1	tablespoon sugar
1/4	cup egg substitute
1/4	cup raisins

Sauce

1	cup vanilla low-fat yogurt

Caramel

1/2	cup sugar
1/8	teaspoon ground cinnamon
2	teaspoons hot water

To Prepare the Pudding

1. In a large saucepan, combine the evaporated milk with 3/4 cup of the 2% milk and the cinnamon stick. Warm over medium-high heat until small bubbles rise around the edge of the pan or a skin starts to form on top of the milk.

2. Combine another 1/4 cup of the 2% milk with the cornmeal and whisk into the hot milk. Stir often until the cornmeal is

thick enough for a spoon to stand upright, about 5 minutes.

3. Combine the cornstarch with the remaining $^1\!/_4$ cup of 2% milk to make a slurry.

4. Add the sugar, egg substitute, and raisins to the cornmeal mixture. Remove from the heat and add the slurry. Return to the burner and stir over medium heat until the mixture thickens again. The pudding is ready when you can move a spoon across the bottom of the pan without the path behind it filling in. This might take up to 5 more minutes, depending on the heat and your pan. Remove and discard the cinnamon stick. Cover the cornmeal mixture to prevent the surface from hardening and set aside until ready to serve.

To Prepare the Sauce

5. Stir the yogurt with a spoon in a small bowl. Do this just before you serve to avoid separation.

To Prepare the Caramel

6. Melt the sugar in a small, heavy-bottomed saucepan over medium-high heat, stirring frequently. When the sugar has melted and turned golden, pull the pan off the heat and add the cinnamon and hot water. Stand back because the water will make the melted sugar bubble vigorously.

7. Turn off the heat and return the pan to the warm burner. You will need to move quickly now, before the caramel sets like hard toffee in the pan.

To Serve

8. Place a generous spoonful of yogurt onto each dessert plate. Scoop $^1\!/_4$ cup or so of the corn pudding into the center of each puddle of yogurt. [An ice cream scoop with a clicker makes this easy.] Using a pointed teaspoon, swirl the caramel over the top in a decorative way. The caramel will harden as soon as it hits the pudding. If the caramel should become too hard, simply warm it again over low heat.

Time Estimate
Hands-on, 30 minutes.

Nutritional Profile per Serving
209 calories; 2 g fat; 1 g saturated fat; 8% of calories from fat;
41 g carbohydrate; 1 g dietary fiber.

Portability
The pudding is easy to prepare ahead and will keep well in an
airtight plastic container. Practice with the caramel beforehand
and plan to prepare it at the party. It is very impressive and lots of
fun when you get it down pat. Pans with hardened caramel are
impossible to wash but will clean themselves miraculously with a
good soaking. Be sure you use a small, heavy-bottomed saucepan,
and don't forget the ice cream scoop!

appetizer
Poached Eggs Cartagena
Bright egg atop a snazzy salsa with black beans and olives. Underneath, a warmed corn tortilla.

main course
Steak Señora Teresita Roman de Zurek
Flank steak broiled in a spiced rub with a tomato pepper sauce.

vegetarian option
Portabella Mushroom Teresita

side dish
Black Rice
Robust rice with a hint of coconut.

vegetable
String Wing Bean Salad
Fresh beans and tomatoes tossed in a warm vinegar glaze laced with fresh basil.

dessert
Meringue Islands with Plum Sauce
Meringue and Italian ladyfingers atop a sea of red plum wine sauce.

travelogue

*O*ur route from St. Thomas to Colombia took us diagonally across the entire Caribbean Sea, following the paths of the ancient Spanish *flotas* on their way to the leading port of call on what was then known as Tierra Firme. Cartagena [pronounced cart-a-hane-a] was founded in 1533 by Don Pedro de Heredia as a base for expeditions in search of El Dorado. The gold, silver, and emeralds that were discovered in the interior were shipped to Cartagena, then loaded on cargo ships bound for Spain. Word of these treasure-laden galleons soon spread, and by the mid-1500s outbound fleets were prime targets for pirates such as Robert Baal and Jack Hawkins. In 1586 Sir Francis Drake, privateering for England, actually took possession of the city and held it for ransom. Before

COLOMBIA
Cool Elegance Under the Mango Trees

Previous page:
Chef and author Señora Teresita Roman de Zurek welcomes us to her shaded garden.

This page, from top:
The Fortress of San Felipe de Barajas looms over Cartagena.
An ancient street marker in the old city [La Ciudad Vieja].
We bid farewell to our gracious hostess.

he sailed for England with his ransom money, he commandeered all the bakeries in the city to bake sea biscuits for his voyage home.

The Spanish responded to the continuing raids by building a network of walls and forts around the city. On an island in the harbor they erected a stone fortress lined with underground tunnels and housed with enough supplies to remain self-sufficient for months. King Philip of Spain, who paid for these monumental fortifications, is said to have looked out his palace window, saying "I am looking for the walls of Cartagena. They cost so much, they must be visible from here."

King Philip would be glad to know that the old walls, over fifty feet thick in some places, are still very much visible today. They enclose the old city [La Ciudad Vieja], now a main attraction for visitors. Narrow cobblestone streets, laid out to catch sea breezes off the bay, open onto small plazas lined with restored houses from the colonial era. Wooden balconies overflow with flowers, and Treena and I could have wandered the crooked streets for hours if we had not been due to meet Señora Teresita Roman de Zurek. The undisputed "Julia Child" of Colombia, she is the highly esteemed author of a number of popular cookbooks which are, regretfully, not yet available in English. We had lunch in her mango-shaded garden, where she entertained us with the gracious hospitality of a Spanish grandee and literally showered us with Colombian specialties. We found a tremendous richness of flavor, color, and aroma in everything we were offered, and Teresita provided me with a great deal of inspiration and a host of ideas for lighter versions of Colombian classics.

For the health-conscious visitor, Cartagena offers a wonderful array of fresh fruit, fine tropical seafood, and a lively attitude towards seasonings. The "foundation foods" of beans and rice offer

Cartagena offers an array of fresh fruit and a lively attitude towards seasonings.

lots of healthy alternatives for culinary explorers who are interested in something more than the familiar meat and potatoes. However, Colombians are very fond of fried foods, animal fats, and coconut oil and this predilection has had a predictable effect on health statistics, with cardiovascular disease accounting for the greatest number of hospital visits among the overall population. In fact, 1989 surveys show that malnutrition and other nutritional disorders were the second and third leading health problems among indigenous people, tuberculosis being the first.

All of this is now beginning to change. Cartagena appears to have escaped the image of Colombia as a drug-infested battlefield and is enjoying a surge of tourists interested in its amenities as a city of complex culture, rich history, and delightful, warm weather. This

Even if you don't have mango trees shading your garden, you can enjoy the calming luxury of this dinner.

increased tourism is bringing new requests for tasty low-fat alternatives, and we found a great deal of evidence of this trend even during our short visit to the city.

As we sailed away from Colombia and up the Isthmus of Panama, the elegance and refinement of the afternoon in the garden of our delightful hostess stayed with us. Even if you don't have mango trees shading your garden, you and your guests can still enjoy the calming luxury of this dinner, which preserves the richness and drama of Colombian cuisine without excessive fats. I am very fond of the appetizer: poached eggs on a bed of bright Colombian salsa. The entreé features flank steak surrounded by a darkened jalapeño sauce, with side dishes of my own black rice and a fresh green bean salad. For dessert we've made a frothy meringue "fortress" for you to float in a rosy fruit sea. The entire menu squeaks in below our 1,000-calorie maximum, with only 19% of calories from fat. The vegetarian version comes in at 728 calories with only 11% of calories from fat.

I've also included directions for making an authentic version of corn water brightened with lemon juice. It reminded me of a lemon barley drink we were given as boys in England. I know it sounds peculiar, but it had a remarkable cooling effect after a hard afternoon of soccer. Colombians don't make very good wine and perhaps because of that and the thirst-provoking climate, they are famous for their soft drinks, which they enjoy with meals rather than drinking alcohol.

This page, from top:
A mango-shaded garden welcomes us to lunch.

This young guest shares the warmth of Colombia charm.

Black rice, a beloved Colombia classic.

Poached Eggs Cartagena

This appetizer is a sort of "huevos rancheros" taken to exciting new levels of flavor, aroma, and texture. The bright, snazzy salsa salutes its Spanish roots with a flourish of green olives, while black beans and cilantro show a South American influence.

Salsa

- 6 large Italian plum tomatoes, such as Roma
- 1 Anaheim chile,* cored, seeded, and finely chopped [1/4 cup]
- 1 1/2 cups cooked black beans [15 ounce or 425-g can], rinsed and drained
- 3 large cloves garlic, peeled, bashed, and chopped [1 tablespoon]
- 3/4 cup sliced green onions
- 12 small stuffed green olives, sliced
- 1/4 teaspoon freshly ground black pepper
- 1/4 teaspoon ground cumin
- 1 teaspoon mild chili powder
- 1/2 teaspoon salt
- 1 tablespoon arrowroot
- 2 tablespoons water
- 4 tablespoons chopped fresh cilantro, 1 tablespoon reserved for garnish

Eggs and Tortillas

- 6 white corn tortillas [6-inch size]
- 6 whole eggs or 1 1/2 cups egg substitute

Garnish

- Chopped fresh cilantro
- 1 teaspoon dried crushed red pepper flakes

1. Preheat the oven to 350 degrees F [180 degrees C]. Take eggs out of refrigerator so they can warm to room temperature.

To Prepare the Salsa

2. Bring a large saucepan of water to a rolling boil. Core the tomatoes and drop them into the boiling water for 1 minute.

[This will loosen the skin enough to peel.] Remove the tomatoes and dip in cold water or allow them to cool on a plate. When the tomatoes are cool, peel and discard skins.

3. Dice the tomatoes and put them into a medium saucepan. Add the chopped chile, black beans, garlic, green onions, olives, pepper, cumin, chili powder, and $1/4$ teaspoon of the salt. Cook for a few minutes over medium heat.

4. Combine the arrowroot with 2 tablespoons of water to make a slurry. Add the slurry to the tomato mixture and stir over medium heat until the salsa is glossy and thickened. Set aside until the eggs are ready, along with 3 tablespoons of the chopped cilantro, which should be added just before serving.

To Prepare the Tortillas and Eggs

5. Oil a large cookie sheet with cooking spray and cover with the tortillas. Spray the tortillas lightly with cooking spray. Warm in the preheated oven for 5 minutes.

6. Add 2 inches of water and the remaining $1/4$ teaspoon of salt to a large, shallow skillet and bring to a simmer. Break an egg into a small dish or saucer and slide gently into the simmering [not boiling] water. Repeat with the rest of the eggs, one by one. When all the eggs have been added, give the pan a gentle "Amtrak" shake to allow the hot water to flow over the tops of the eggs and cook them lightly. [Keep the water just barely simmering.] After about 4 minutes, the whites should be firm and the yolks should be runny. Serve immediately.

7. If you choose to use egg substitute, heat a medium skillet over medium-low heat. Spray with cooking spray and pour in the egg substitute. When the eggs start to set, push gently with a spatula, moving the cooked part to the center of the pan and letting the uncooked part run to the bottom of the pan. It is important that the eggs stay soft and glossy. They can be ruined by overcooking or overstirring.

To Serve

8. Stir the 3 tablespoons of cilantro into the thickened salsa.

Place a hot tortilla on each warmed salad plate and spoon a healthy dollop of the salsa into the middle of the tortilla. Top with a poached egg or a $^{1}/_{4}$-cup scoop of the scrambled eggs. For garnish, sprinkle the chopped cilantro and red pepper flakes over the eggs. Offer more pepper flakes in a small dish for those who like it more than just hot.

Time Estimate
Hands-on, 40 minutes.

Nutritional Profile per Serving
188 calories; 7 g fat; 2 g saturated fat; 34% of calories from fat; 22 g carbohydrate; 4 g dietary fiber.

For Special Needs
To reduce the saturated fat content to zero, replace the 6 whole eggs with $1^{1}/_{2}$ cups of egg substitute.

Nutritional Profile per Serving with Egg Substitute
131 calories; 2 g fat; 0 g saturated fat; 10% of calories from fat; 22 g carbohydrate; 4 g dietary fiber.

Portability
Make the salsa ahead and transport in a plastic container. Reheat in a microwave or small saucepan and stir in the fresh chopped cilantro just before serving. Take the tortillas, raw eggs, and a skillet along with you to prepare the eggs just before serving.

Steak Señora Teresita Roman de Zurek
Flank Steak Broiled in a Spiced Rub with a Tomato Jalapeño Sauce

Cattle play a small but vital part in Colombian agriculture, and there is a great liking for a "sobrebarriga" when entertaining visitors. A spicy rub gives the beef lots of flavor, and a tomato and jalepeño sauce provides the perfect accent. My adaptation is named in honor of our lovely and gracious hostess. Black Rice [page 72] and String Bean Salad [page 73] complete this Colombian dinner.

Steak

1½	pounds [675 g] flank steak, trimmed of all visible fat
4	cloves garlic, peeled, bashed, and finely chopped
¼	cup finely chopped sweet onion
1	jalapeño pepper,* cored, seeded, and finely diced [1½ tablespoons]
1	Italian plum tomato, such as Roma, cored, seeded, and finely diced
⅛	teaspoon powdered bay leaf
¼	teaspoon cayenne pepper
⅛	teaspoon ground allspice
¼	teaspoon salt
½	teaspoon light olive oil

Tomato Jalapeño Sauce

½	teaspoon light olive oil
2	cups roughly chopped sweet onion
3	jalapeño peppers, cored, seeded, and roughly chopped
3	small [or 2 large] Italian plum tomatoes, such as Roma, quartered
1	can [14½ ounces or 411 g] crushed tomatoes in purée
⅛	teaspoon salt
⅛	teaspoon ground allspice
¼	teaspoon powdered bay leaf
1	tablespoon arrowroot
2	tablespoons water

*Handling Hot Peppers

*Handling Hot Peppers

The membranes and seeds of hot chiles contain capsaicin, the chemical compound that gives chile peppers their heat. If this chemical ends up anywhere besides your tongue, it can be quite irritating. I suggest wearing rubber gloves while you're working with hot peppers; if not, scrub your hands with soap and water afterward. If you only need a few tablespoons of minced chile for a recipe, cut out a portion of one side, leaving the rest of the pepper [with the seeds and membranes] intact. You'll find the chile stays fresher while stored in a plastic bag in the refrigerator, and you'll handle fewer seeds.

Vegetarian Option [*per Serving*]

    3 medium portabella mushroom caps

    $1/2$ teaspoon olive oil

    1 tablespoon fresh lemon juice

1. Put the flank steak in a shallow dish and spread the chopped garlic, onion, jalapeño, and diced tomato over the top. Sprinkle with the bay, cayenne, allspice, and salt. Using the flat side of a large knife, massage the mixture into the meat. Set the steak aside to absorb the flavors.

2. While the beef is marinating, make the sauce. Warm the oil in a medium frying pan over medium heat. Sauté the onions until slightly browned, 3 to 5 minutes. Stir in the jalapeños, tomatoes [both fresh and canned], salt, allspice, and bay leaf. Cook for 10 minutes over low heat. Cover and set aside. [Vegetarian Option: Set aside $1/4$ cup of sauce per vegetarian serving before proceeding.]

3. Preheat the broiler.

4. Warm a large frying pan over high heat and add $1/2$ teaspoon of the oil. Lay the flank steak in the pan and brown for 1 minute. Tilt the frying pan and slide the flank steak onto the rack of a broiler pan, browned side down. Set aside the frying pan but do not clean it. Spray the top of the flank steak with cooking spray and broil for 10 minutes, until it is crusted on top but still pink in the middle.

5. While the steak is broiling, finish preparing the sauce. Pour $1/2$ cup of water into the frying pan where the steak was browned and stir to remove the flavorful bits of meat from the bottom of the pan. Pour this liquid into a medium saucepan. Press the tomato sauce through a sieve into the same saucepan, discarding the pulp.

6. Combine the arrowroot with 2 tablespoons of water to make a slurry. Add the slurry to the sauce and stir over medium heat until thickened. Remove from the heat until ready to serve.

7. Transfer the flank steak to a large plate, making sure not to

lose any of the flavorful juices. Press the topping flat with a spatula or wide knife. Carve the steak into thin slices, cutting diagonally across the grain. Pour the juices from the broiler pan and the plate into the tomato sauce.

8. To serve, lay three thin slices of meat on each warmed plate and top with a generous spoonful of tomato sauce. Serve Black Rice and String Bean Salad alongside.

Time Estimate
Hands-on, 40 minutes.

Nutritional Profile per Serving
270 calories; 10 g fat; 4 g saturated fat; 32% of calories from fat; 18 g carbohydrate; 4 g dietary fiber.

Vegetarian Option: Portabella Mushroom Teresita
Sauté the mushroom caps in the oil and lemon juice over medium-high heat for about 2 minutes per side, or until soft. Serve with the 1/4 cup of reserved tomato sauce.

Vegetarian Option Nutritional Profile per Serving
130 calories; 4 g fat; 0 g saturated fat; 23% of calories from fat; 23 g carbohydrate; 4 g dietary fiber.

Black Rice...Well, Almost!

The popular Colombian classic—without excessive saturated fats.

- 1/2 teaspoon light olive oil
- 1/2 cup finely chopped onion
- 1 cup long-grain white rice
- 1/4 teaspoon cayenne pepper
- 1/8 teaspoon ground allspice
- 1 1/2 teaspoons coconut essence
- 2 cups low-sodium beef or vegetable stock*
- 1 can [15 ounces or 425 g] black beans, drained
- 2 tablespoons fresh lime juice

1. Preheat the oven to 450 degrees F [230 degrees C].

2. Warm the oil in a large frying pan over medium heat. Sauté the onion for 2 minutes until soft. Stir in the rice and sauté for an additional 2 minutes. Add the cayenne, allspice, and 1/2 teaspoon of the coconut essence. Cook long enough to warm the spices, then remove from the heat.

3. Transfer the rice to an ovenproof baking dish, approximately 8 inches square, and cover with the stock. [Vegetarian Option: Use vegetable stock here.] Bake in the preheated oven for 20 minutes.

4. When the rice is done, remove from the oven and stir in the black beans, lime juice, and the remaining teaspoon of coconut essence. Keep warm.

Time Estimate
Hands-on, 10 minutes; unsupervised, 20 minutes.

Nutritional Profile per Serving
157 calories; 1 g fat; 0 g saturated fat; 3% of calories from fat; 34 g carbohydrate; 4 g dietary fiber.

Vegetarian Option
Replace the beef stock with low-sodium vegetable stock.

String Wing Bean Salad

Wing beans, which take their name from wing-like flanges along their pods, are prolific growers in humid equatorial zones. If you can find them fresh in your produce market, they are well worth trying. [Choose small pods for the best flavor.] If wing beans are not available, fresh green beans will work beautifully in this wonderful salad-type vegetable dish.

Salad

- 1 pound [450 g] green beans or wing beans, tipped, tailed, and cut in half
- 1/4 teaspoon salt
- 1/4 teaspoon freshly ground black pepper
- 1/8 teaspoon ground allspice
- 4 fresh Italian plum tomatoes, such as Roma, cut lengthwise into eighths
- 1/4 cup roughly chopped stuffed green olives
- 6 fresh basil leaves, finely sliced [1 tablespoon]
- 2 green onions, sliced into 1/4-inch [3/4-cm] pieces [1/4 cup]

Glaze

- 1/4 cup balsamic or red wine vinegar
- 1/4 teaspoon arrowroot
- 1/2 teaspoon water

To Prepare the Salad

1. Place the beans in a large vegetable steamer and sprinkle with the salt, pepper, and allspice. Cover and steam for 5 minutes.

2. Combine the tomatoes, olives, basil, and onions in a large serving bowl and set aside.

To Prepare the Glaze

3. Combine the arrowroot with 1/2 teaspoon of water to make a slurry. Pour the vinegar into a small saucepan and add the slurry. Stir over medium heat until clear, glossy, and slightly thickened.

•Colombian Corn Water

This is a drink which we were served on a hot summer evening in Colombia. Colombians are much more likely to drink corn water or soft drinks with their meals than alcohol, so this beverage will add an authentic flavor to your Colombian dinner.

    1   cup masa harina
    7   cups water
    1   cup fresh lemon juice [4 large
        lemons], rinds reserved
    6   tablespoons sugar
    1   bottle of club soda

1. In a large bowl, whisk together the masa harina, 4 cups of the water, and the lemon juice. Cut the lemon rinds in half and add to the masa water. Let the mixture stand for 2 hours, and then strain through cheesecloth or muslin into a medium saucepan.

2. Stir in the sugar and the remaining 3 cups of water. Bring the mixture to the boil, then reduce the heat and simmer for 10 minutes.

3. Serve warm or ice cold with enough soda water to give it some fizz.

To Serve

4. Add the cooked beans to the salad bowl and toss with the warm vinegar glaze. Serve immediately.

Time Estimate

Hands-on, 10 minutes.

Nutritional Profile per Serving

49 calories; 1 g fat; 0 g saturated fat; 19% of calories from fat; 9 g carbohydrate; 4 g dietary fiber.

Meringue Islands with Plum Sauce

The fruit in Colombia is truly magnificent, and the variety is astounding. I often think of the afternoon Treena and I spent in Señora de Zurek's beautiful garden, where huge mangoes sagged from hundred-year-old branches. Another fragrant fruit with yellow-orange globes is the mammee, or South American apricot. Mammees are native to Colombia, and their rosy flesh is somewhat like red plums in flavor. If you can't find mammees, any deep red plum [like Friar or Santa Rosa] will substitute in this spectacular dessert, where a crisp meringue floats upon a plum sauce like an iceberg on a "wine dark sea" [with apologies to Patrick O'Brian].

Meringue

- 1/4 cup plus 6 tablespoons granulated sugar
- 4 large egg whites, at room temperature
- 1/4 teaspoon cream of tartar
- 1/2 teaspoon vanilla extract
- 12 low-fat ladyfingers or Italian *savoiardi** biscuits

Plum Sauce

- 4 mammees* or dark red plums, such as Friar [1 pound or 450 g]
- 1 cup slightly sweet white wine [I prefer dealcoholized Ariel blanc]
- 1 1/2 tablespoons brown sugar
- 1 teaspoon fresh lemon juice

Garnish

Fresh mint leaves

To Prepare the Meringue

1. Make sure the egg whites are at room temperature before beginning the recipe. Preheat the oven to 350 degrees F [180 degrees C] and position a rack in the center of the oven. Spray a 6-cup capacity loaf pan [either glass or nonstick metal] with cooking spray.

2. Melt 1/4 cup of the sugar in a small saucepan over medium-high heat, shaking the pan occasionally, until the sugar melts and

*Savoiardi

These crisp Italian ladyfingers are low in fat, mild in flavor, and keep their shape. This makes them ideal for low-fat desserts as well as by themselves with tea or coffee. Look for the Ferrara brand in a specialty food store or contact:

Calavati
2537 Brunswick Avenue
Lynden, NY 07036
[908] 651-7600

*Mammees

If you are unable to find this fruit locally, you may order it during summer months from:

Robert Is Here
19900 S.W. 344th Street
Homestead, FL 33034-1408
[305] 246-1592

turns brown, about 3 minutes. Pour the caramel into the bottom of the prepared loaf pan and quickly tip the pan back and forth until the bottom is completely covered. The caramel will harden almost immediately.

3. Make sure the mixing bowl and whip are perfectly clean and grease-free. Beat the whites on low speed until frothy, then add the cream of tartar. Increase the speed to high and beat until soft peaks begin to form. Gradually sprinkle in the sugar, 1 tablespoon at a time, until all 6 tablespoons have been added. Beat on high speed until stiff peaks form, about 2 minutes. Beat in the vanilla.

4. Spread a third of the meringue over the caramel in the bottom of the prepared baking pan. Trim the ends of 6 of the ladyfingers or *savoiardis* so that they will fit across the width of the pan. Lay them side-by-side on top of the meringue layer. Spread half the remaining meringue over the cookies, using a rubber spatula to fill the crevices between the cookies. Rap the loaf pan on the counter to release any air bubbles. Repeat the cookie layer with the remaining 6 whole cookies, which should fit across the top of the pan without cutting. Spread the remaining meringue over the cookies for the final layer, again pressing into the crevices and tapping to release air.

5. Place a large baking pan in the oven and partially fill with boiling water to create a water bath for the meringue. Set the loaf pan in the center of the baking pan and adjust the water level to reach halfway up the sides. Bake the meringue for 30 minutes, then take a look in the oven. If the top is getting too brown, cover loosely with foil. Bake for an additional 15 minutes, for a total of 45 minutes.

6. Remove the pan from the oven and run a wet knife along the sides of the pan to loosen the meringue. Invert onto a large plate and allow to cool. When ready to serve, cut into 6 pieces with a wet knife.

7. Cut the plums into quarters and discard the pits. Combine the plums and wine in a large saucepan and roughly mash the fruit with a fork. Bring the mixture to a boil over high heat. Continue to mash the plums occasionally while the sauce is coming to the boil, which should take 2 or 3 minutes. Reduce the heat and simmer, uncovered, for about 15 minutes.

8. Pour the sauce into a blender and process for 1 minute. Press the purée through a strainer into a medium saucepan, discarding any remaining pulp. Add the brown sugar and lemon juice and cook over low heat until the sugar dissolves.

To Serve

9. Spoon a puddle of plum sauce onto a dessert plate and top with a slice of the baked meringue. Garnish with mint leaves.

Time Estimate

Hands-on, 20 minutes; unsupervised, 45 minutes.

Nutritional Profile per Serving

189 calories; 1 g fat; 0 g saturated fat; 4% of calories from fat; 42 g carbohydrate; 1 g dietary fiber.

Portability

Bake the meringue in the afternoon and take it with you in its loaf pan, then unmold it just before serving. For added drama, whip the whites at the gathering and bake the meringue before their very eyes. If you make the meringue at the party, take along a sprayed loaf pan with the hardened caramel already in it. The plum sauce can be made ahead.

appetizer

Broiled Shrimp with Chile Sauce Barra Vieja

Shrimp broiled with a tomato and chile sauce, served with a garlic yogurt "mayonnaise."

main dish

Posole

Classic Mexican stew with hominy, chicken, and pork.

vegetarian option

Posole with Red Kidney Beans

dessert

Pineapple Nieve

Snowy white ice drenched in lime and pineapple.

travelogue

*A*fter a peaceful sleep on our last night in the calm waters of the Caribbean, Treena and I awoke early for our trip through the Panama Canal. Soon we were watching deckhands expertly encouraging the Queen Elizabeth II to slip through the locks with only six inches to spare on each side. I shall cease complaining about our garage at home!

We emerged from the canal into the Pacific and headed north up the coast of Central America toward Mexico and our next destination: Acapulco! As the QE II nudged into the bay, Treena and I relived many fond memories of this beautiful place. During our Galloping Gourmet days of the 1970s, our quest for gourmet experiences took us to Mexico City, Acapulco, and down the Pacific coast to visit Las Brisas and the legendary Hungarian hotelier, Henry Brandstetter. Two decades later, we were on a similar journey with a different focus—this time we were searching for the same excitement in food and flavors, but without some of the temptations of the past.

Much has changed in this part of Mexico since our first visit. Today's Acapulco is lively, modern, and crowded during peak

ACAPULCO
Golden Sands and the Deep Blue Sea

season. I know people who remember when this was a sleepy fishing village with a few guest houses decorating its sandy shores, a hideaway for Hollywood stars; now it is a popular getaway for thousands of sun-starved northerners. But it is still breathtakingly beautiful. The foothills of the majestic Sierra Madre Mountains rise directly from the harbor, and steep cliffs plunge straight into the sea. In pre-Hispanic times this bay was home to the Nahuatl Indians, and its name derives from their words *Acatl*, "place of canes", *Pol* "to break," and *Co* "a place." The Nahuatls also gave us the word *chillis* for the hot peppers that grow in their homeland.

We were greeted in Acapulco by Señora Susanna Palazuelos, author of the *Mexico the Beautiful Cookbook*. She promptly whisked us off for an afternoon of adventure. We left the grand sweep of the bay and its high-rise hotels and headed south on the Carretera Escenica [scenic highway] into forested hills. We topped a ridge and wound down a steep headland to the elegant Camino Real Resort, where we enjoyed a leisurely breakfast with Leon Borenstein, the general manager of this wonderful place. One of the epicurean treats on the menu was *huitlachoche*, a black fungus that grows on ears of corn. Even though it sounds rather alarming, it was quite delicious,

Popular with sun-starved northerners, it is still breathtakingly beautiful.

with a velvety smooth texture and a delicate, exotic flavor. Mr. Borenstein explained that this highly prized fungus is one of the world's rarest foods. It cannot be cultivated and only appears under certain conditions during the rainy season.

Our next course was *huachinango a la talla*, red snapper grilled over charcoal and liberally basted on one side with a tomato and chile sauce and on the other with garlic mayonnaise. We finished the last of the fresh corn tortillas and relaxed on the terrace. Our view overlooking the gleaming blue bay and its golden sand beach seemed to inspire grand discussions of food, health, and history. I was struck by the sense of passion Mr. Borenstein had for his work and for the culture of Mexico. I believe we will hear much more about this man in the future.

I was ready to settle down underneath one of the white beach canopies for a siesta, but our hostess had other plans in mind. Our next destination was Barra Vieja, a small village south of Acapulco, well off the beaten track. There we had lunch in a *palapas*, a

restaurant with open sides and a thatched roof. You don't really need walls in this climate, and it was refreshing to sit in the open air next to a sandy lagoon lined with palm and banana trees. Hammocks hung near our table, inspiring Treena to remark that this must be a place for real swingers.

Barra Vieja is said to be the source of the popular dish *huachinango a la talla*. We had already tried this at Camino Real and, of course,

> *My fish was so fresh that I am sure it had just been unloaded from one of the fishing boats that rocked in the lagoon...*

we had to sample the local version, which was garnished with a more robust chile sauce. My fish was so fresh that I am sure it had just been unloaded from one of the fishing boats that rocked in the lagoon, waiting for their next foray into the great fishing grounds of the Pacific.

Over lunch we talked with Susanna and Eduardo about the rich culinary history of this region, including its most famous inland dish, the hearty *posole*. This substantial stew is based on pork, and old recipes call for a whole pig's head—and feet. Sometimes chicken is added as well, plus plenty of vegetables and hominy. Susanna said that this stew did not always include hominy, which was usually used for making tortillas. One year a senior churchman announced plans to visit the village of Chilapa in the mountains above Acapulco. A huge feast was planned. The women soaked dried corn and cooked it in water and lime to make the hominy [*nixtamal*], which they would then drain and grind into masa for the tortillas. Unfortunately, they underestimated the labor needed to grind enough masa to make thousands of tortillas. Instead, they opted to put the large kernels of soft golden hominy directly into their stew made of pork and poultry. It was a hit and has remained so ever since.

I think our version of this dish will also be a hit with your guests when you serve this dinner from the heart of southern Mexico. Have your favorite fishing boat bring in some fresh shrimp for our appetizer of grilled shrimp basted with a tomato-chile sauce and my own yogurt garlic "mayonnaise." The entrée is *posole*, of course, made with chicken, pork, and a marvelous array of seasonings. The dessert is a cool pineapple ice served with brittle cinnamon tortilla chips, the perfect foil for a meal full of such earthy flavors.

Previous page:
A Panama hat puts anyone in the holiday spirit
We slip through the Panama Canal with inches to spare.

Facing page, from top:
Bright skies and brisk breezes welcome us to Acapulco.
Horsing around on board the QE II.
Acapulco is lively during peak tourist season.

This page, from top:
Picturesque Acapulco brings back fond memories.
Eduardo Palazuelos, one of our gracious hosts.
We hope this little guy isn't headed for *posole*.

travelogue 5. ACAPULCO

Our Acapulco evening totals fewer than 800 calories and only 15 grams of fat. The vegetarian menu uses small sweet carrots in lieu of shrimp, which brings the totals down below 600 calories and 7 grams of fat.

If you like, you can accompany dessert with a cup of traditional Mexican hot chocolate thickened with masa, a drink descended from Mayan Indians [although if you wish to be truly authentic you will have to add chili powder as well]. When served with the crisp cinnamon chips and the pineapple ice, the warm chocolate sets off an extraordinary contrast between hot and cold, sweet and tart, crisp and smooth. These are the sort of taste combinations that make it possible to eat wonderful, satisfying food with very little fat.

I live in hope for the warm, wonderfully hospitable and caring people of Mexico. Theirs is a rich, colorful history—they've contributed much to the food world, and conceivably, the future will be just as bright. At the present time, heart disease is the leading cause of death in Mexico. I hope that, because the food of Mexico is full of such aroma, color, and flavor, that a lighter, more varied, and less saturated fat-based cuisine will soon emerge.

Broiled Shrimp with Chile Sauce Barra Vieja

There are many versions of the red snapper dish called "Huachinango a la Talla," and I sampled an especially delicious rendition in the small village of Barra Vieja. Grilled over an open wood fire, the fish was covered with a rich crust of tomatoes, red peppers, and mayonnaise. For this appetizer, I replaced the snapper with jumbo shrimp, but I preserved the robust flavors of the delicious chile sauce.

SERVES 6

Chile Sauce

- 6 dried New Mexico chiles
- 3 ancho chiles
- 3 cloves garlic, peeled, bashed, and chopped
- 2/3 cup chopped onion
- 4 Italian plum tomatoes, such as Roma, quartered
- 1/2 teaspoon ground cumin
- 1/2 teaspoon dried marjoram
- 1/2 teaspoon dried oregano
- 1/8 teaspoon ground cloves
- 1/4 teaspoon salt
- 1 tablespoon white distilled vinegar
- 1 tablespoon molasses

Yogurt Mayonnaise

- 1/2 cup yogurt cheese [page 37]
- 1 tablespoon fresh lime juice
- 1 pinch of powdered saffron
- 1/4 teaspoon salt

Other Ingredients

- 24 cherry tomatoes
- 6 medium shrimp [about 2 ounces or 55 g each]
- 1 bunch watercress, thoroughly washed

Garnish

- 1 teaspoon mild chili powder
- 1 tablespoon chopped fresh cilantro
- 6 corn tortillas

Vegetarian Option [per Serving]

   2 ounces [55 g] 2¼-inch [5-cm] baby carrots

1. To prepare the New Mexico and ancho chiles, remove the stems and slice the chiles open lengthwise. Remove the seeds and pulp with the tip of a knife blade or a small spoon. Put the chiles in a saucepan with 1 cup of water and bring to a boil. Turn off the heat, cover, and let soak for 10 minutes.

2. While the chiles are soaking, make the yogurt mayonnaise. Whisk together the yogurt cheese, lime juice, saffron, and salt. Cover and set aside.

3. To finish the chile sauce, strain the soaked chiles, reserving the liquid. Transfer the chiles to a food processor or blender. Add the garlic, onion, tomatoes, cumin, marjoram, oregano, cloves, salt, vinegar, and molasses. Pulse, then blend until smooth, about 4 minutes. Transfer the sauce to a small saucepan. Rinse the processor bowl or blender jar with 1 cup of the pepper-soaking liquid and stir into the sauce. Bring to a boil over medium heat, then lower heat and simmer for 15 minutes.

4. Meanwhile, warm a medium frying pan over medium-high heat. Cook the cherry tomatoes until lightly browned on the outside. Transfer the tomatoes to a plate and gently mash with a fork. Remove most of the seeds.

5. Preheat the broiler.

6. Peel the shrimp, leaving the tail shell attached. Slit each shrimp lengthwise down the center, being careful not to cut all the way through. Remove the sand-filled vein and open the shrimp out flat, like a butterfly. Weave a toothpick through the thickest part of the meat, so that the two halves of the shrimp remain flat. Brush each shrimp generously on both sides with the chile sauce. Place the shrimp on a broiler pan and broil for 3 minutes on each side. Serve immediately.

7. To serve, divide the watercress among small salad plates. Arrange three crushed tomatoes and one shrimp on top of the

watercress. Spoon a little chile sauce over each shrimp and top with a dollop of yogurt mayonnaise. Dust with mild chili powder and garnish with the chopped cilantro and hot tortillas.

Time Estimate

Hands-on, 30 minutes.

Nutritional Profile per Serving

172 calories; 2 g fat; 0 g saturated fat; 10% of calories from fat; 23 g carbohydrate; 3 g dietary fiber.

Vegetarian Option

Replace the shrimp with baby carrots [you could call them "garden prawns"], steamed for 6 to 8 minutes, or until tender but still crisp. Coat the carrots with 1/2 cup of the chile sauce and serve over watercress and tomatoes.

Vegetarian Option Nutritional Profile per Serving

135 calories; 1 g fat; 0 g saturated fat; 6% of calories from fat; 27 g carbohydrate; 4 g dietary fiber.

Portability

Prepare the chile sauce and yogurt mayonnaise ahead and carry them in plastic containers. Peel, devein, and lace the shrimp on toothpicks. The tomatoes, watercress, and whole cilantro can travel in resealable bags, but wait to chop the cilantro until just before you need it. The tortillas can stay in their package until ready to heat in the microwave or oven. If one or more of the guests is vegetarian, take the carrots raw and steam them shortly before serving.

*Hominy

Hominy kernels look somewhat like popcorn and have a soft, chewy consistency. Hominy is sold either in canned or dried form. The canned version has a very high salt content so you may want to try to find it dry. One mail order source is:

Indian Harvest
Specialty Foods, Inc.
P.O. Box 428
Bemidji, MN 56619-0428

[800] 294-2433.

Posole

"Posole" [or "pozole"] is an earthy Mexican stew that combines hominy with broth, meats, and the chef's special touches, usually pork and spices. The one constant ingredient is hominy, which traditional Mexican cooks spend two days preparing by pounding and soaking white corn kernels [called "maiz para posole"]. I opted for canned hominy instead. I've also given more focus to chicken than you might ordinarily find and, I hope, created a dish with a great deal of hearty richness and much less fat than the traditional version. Serve this stew with hot corn tortillas.

SERVES 6

- 1 1/2 pounds [675 g] pork spareribs
- 1/8 plus 1/4 teaspoon salt
- 1/4 teaspoon freshly ground black pepper
- 1 chicken [about 3 1/2 pounds or 1 1/2 kg]
- 1/2 teaspoon light olive oil
- 1 medium onion, roughly chopped [about 1 cup]
- 2 cloves garlic, peeled, bashed, and chopped
- 3 bay leaves
- 1 can [29 ounces or 812 g] yellow hominy,* rinsed and drained
- 1 bunch fresh kale, heavy stalks removed, thoroughly washed, and torn into 1-inch [2 1/2-cm] pieces [8 cups]

Garnish
- 1/2 cup fresh oregano leaves
- 3 limes, halved
- 1/4 cup dried crushed red pepper flakes
- 1/2 cup finely diced onion
- 6 corn tortillas

Vegetarian Option [per Serving]
- 1 cup low-fat vegetable stock
- 1/2 cup hominy
- 1 cup kale, torn into 1-inch [2 1/2-cm] pieces
- 3 heaping tablespoons cooked kidney beans
- 1 tablespoon grated Parmesan cheese

1. Preheat the oven to 350 degrees F [180 degrees C].

2. Season the ribs with ⅛ teaspoon of the salt and the pepper and place on a rack in a roasting pan. Add 1 cup of water to the pan and roast in the preheated oven for 1¼ hours, or until tender.

3. Rinse the chicken well and pat dry. Warm the oil in a Dutch oven or large iron casserole over medium-high heat. Sauté the onion and garlic until the onion starts to soften, about 2 minutes. Lay the chicken on top of the onion and pour ½ cup of water over the chicken. Cover and continue cooking for an additional 3 minutes. The chicken should be firm and white on the outside.

4. Turn the chicken over and cover with 10 cups of hot water. Add the bay leaves and remaining ¼ teaspoon of salt. Bring the liquid to a boil, reduce the heat, and cover the pot. Simmer for 1 hour. Turn off the heat, leave covered, and let sit for 20 minutes.

5. After the pork ribs have roasted, transfer them to a cutting board to cool. Add a little water to the roasting pan and deglaze with a flat-ended spurtle or wooden spoon, then pour the liquid into the pot with the chicken. Cut the meat off the ribs and roughly dice into ¼-inch [¾-cm] pieces, or smaller.

6. Transfer the chicken to a large plate. Remove the skin and return it to the pot. Separate the legs and wings from the bird and return the wings to the pot. Roughly chop the leg and thigh meat into pieces that can be eaten easily with a soup spoon. Remove the breast meat and cut into neat ½-inch cubes.

7. Return the carcass and any juices from the carving plate to the pot, along with the pork bones. Bring the stock to a vigorous boil for a few minutes to reduce the liquid by 50% and concentrate the flavors. Pour into a fat strainer a few cups at a time and allow the fat to rise to the surface. Pour the de-fatted stock [you should have about 5 cups] into a large pot. Add the hominy, kale, pork, and chicken meat. [Vegetarian Option: Set aside ½ cup hominy and 1 cup kale per vegetarian

serving.] Simmer for 5 minutes.

8. To serve, divide the *posole* among six warmed soup bowls. Pass small dishes of the fresh oregano leaves, lime halves, red pepper flakes, and diced onion for your guests to add according to their own tastes. Pass a basket of hot corn tortillas.

Time Estimate
Hands-on, 30 minutes; unsupervised, 1 hour and 20 minutes.

Nutritional Profile per Serving
398 calories; 11 g fat; 3 g saturated fat; 23% of calories from fat; 43 g carbohydrate; 8 g dietary fiber.

Vegetarian Option: Posole with Red Kidney Beans
About 10 minutes before serving, bring the vegetable stock to a boil in a medium saucepan. Add the reserved hominy and kale and the kidney beans and simmer for 5 minutes. Add the grated Parmesan cheese and serve in a warmed bowl. Garnish as you would the *posole*.

Vegetarian Option Nutritional Profile per Serving
265 calories; 4 g fat; 1 g saturated fat; 13% of calories from fat; 49 g carbohydrate; 9 g dietary fiber.

Pineapple Nieve

SERVES 6

Nieve is the Spanish word for snow, and when you taste this extraordinary ice you'll see why I gave it this name. Each bite literally feels like a clump of freshly fallen snow drenched in lime and pineapple. It's hard to imagine a more refreshing end to a meal, and what an incredible "collision" with the hot chocolate drink [page 90] and Cinnamon Chips [page 91] that I recommend you serve alongside!

Serves 6

1 whole fresh pineapple*
1/4 cup fresh lime juice
1/4 cup granulated sugar

1. Either peel or core the pineapple depending upon whether you want to use the shell as a serving dish for the *nieve*. If it is to be used, immediately put the hollowed husk in the freezer.

2. Chop the fruit into rough chunks. Process them in a food processor for about 2 minutes, or until there are no whole pieces left. Add the lime juice and sugar and blend for another 15 seconds, until well mixed. If you can still see thin strings of pineapple pulp, press or rub the mixture through a mesh strainer.

3. Freeze the fruit sauce in an ice cream machine, following the manufacturer's directions. If you don't have an ice cream machine, freeze the liquid in a shallow baking pan in your freezer until it is almost solid. This will take an hour or two depending on your freezer. Once it is frozen, remove from the freezer and break into small pieces. Put the pieces in the large bowl of an electric mixer and beat until smooth. Return the mixture to the shallow pan and refreeze. Repeat the freezing and beating process until you are satisfied with the consistency of the ice. The more times you beat, the smoother the texture will be. One short beating will produce a granita. Several beatings will result in a richer, smoother texture.

•Cutting Pineapple

To prepare a pineapple shell for filling, use a long serrated knife and make a flat cut across the top of the pineapple to remove the leaves and a portion of the top. Leave the bottom intact. Using a sharp knife with at least a 5-inch blade, cut around the inside of the shell, just deep enough to separate the flesh from the shell. Go around the perimeter a couple of times to be sure the flesh is completely loosened from the rind. Turn the pineapple on its side. Insert the knife into the base and work it around inside each side to loosen the flesh from the rind. Remove the pineapple flesh, pulling the rind out in one piece. Cut the flesh lengthwise into 4 wedges and remove the coarse core. Rinse out the shell and freeze until firm. Set the shell upright in a cake pan to fill.

dessert 5. ACAPULCO

Warm Chocolate Drink

Ending a meal with this warm drink is a Mexican tradition that is quite satisfying. I've used hot chocolate mix instead of dark chocolate because there is less fat per cup. If you were in Mexico, water thickened with masa might be used. It thickens the drink somewhat and adds a slight flavor you may recognize as the taste of corn tortillas. It's totally optional here and the combination can be described as an acquired taste.

> 1/3 cup masa harina [optional]
> 4 cups water
> 1/4 teaspoon ground cinnamon
> 2 individual serving-size packages or equivalent nonfat hot chocolate mix
> 1 tablespoon brown sugar

Garnish: Cinnamon sticks

1. Whisk the masa harina and 2 cups of the water in a medium sauce pan. Let the mixture stand for 15 minutes. Strain the liquid three times through a fine sieve or cheesecloth, pouring it back and forth between two saucepans to remove the bulk of the corn residue. Shake the sieve, but do not force the masa through.

2. Heat the strained liquid in a medium saucepan over medium heat, and add the remaining 2 cups of water and the cinnamon. When the liquid is hot but not boiling, stir in the hot cocoa mix. Heat, just below a boil, for 30 seconds. Whisk just before serving.

4. When you are satisfied with the texture, let the ice ripen in the freezer for 30 minutes. Then it is ready to serve or pack into the frozen pineapple shell.

5. To serve, scoop the ice into small stemmed dessert dishes or present in the frozen husk. Serve with Cinnamon Chips and a cup of Warm Chocolate Drink.

Time Estimate
Hands-on, 10 minutes; unsupervised, 1 hour.

Nutritional Profile per Serving
74 calories; 0 g fat; 0 g saturated fat; 4% of calories from fat; 19 g carbohydrate; 1 g dietary fiber.

Portability
If you made the *nieve* in a ice cream maker, carry it to the party in the insulated insert in a large resealable bag. If not, transfer the ice to a plastic container to ripen and then wrap it in several layers of newspaper, a very good insulator. Put the ice in the freezer as soon as you get to the party. If it has frozen very hard, remove and set on the kitchen counter when the main course is served so it will be "scoopable" by dessert time. The chips can be carried in a resealable bag or plastic container.

Cinnamon Chips

These crisp, sweet chips are easy to make and a delightful
accompaniment to fruit ices of all kinds. They make great after-school
snacks as well.

  1   tablespoon sugar
  1/4   teaspoon ground cinnamon
  2   flour tortillas, [8-inch or 20-cm size]

1. Preheat the oven to 350 degrees F [180 degrees C].

2. Combine the sugar and cinnamon in a small bowl or shaker.
   Lay the tortillas on a cutting board and spray with water until
   they are wet but not soaked. Sprinkle the cinnamon-sugar
   mixture over the top and cut each tortilla into 12 wedges.

3. Arrange the wedges in a single layer on a baking tray and bake
   for 15 minutes, or until crisp. Transfer to a rack to cool. The
   chips will stay crisp for several days in an airtight container.

Time Estimate
Hands-on, 5 minutes; unsupervised, 15 minutes.

Nutritional Profile per Serving
46 calories; 1 g fat; 0 g saturated fat; 16% of calories from fat;
9 g carbohydrate; 0 g dietary fiber.

soup
Corn Chowder
Fresh kernels scraped from the cob and smoothed into a creamy soup.

main dish
Duck Breasts in Plum Sauce
A citrus marinade on a pan-seared, oven-roasted duck breast served with a rich plum sauce.

vegetarian option
Acorn Squash with Citrus and Garbanzos

vegetable
Celery Root and Potato Purée
The satisfying comfort of potatoes deepened with the flavors of celeriac.

salad
Mesclun Salad with Fruit
Delicate fresh salad with bright notes of fresh fruit.

dessert
Orange Chocolate Yogurt Cake
Moist yogurt chocolate cake with flavorful orange sauce.

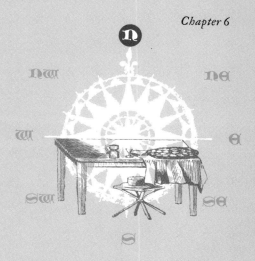

travelogue

*T*reena and I were looking forward to setting foot on U.S. shores as we sailed smoothly out of Acapulco Bay and headed up the Pacific coast, bound for City of Angels. Before relocating to the cloudy Northwest, Treena and I spent a good deal of time in California and we were anxious to see how things had changed. When we disembarked in Los Angeles, we were met by Susan Bowerman, a gifted Registered Dietitian associated with the National Physicians Network. Susan loaded us into her car and we set off into the traffic.

It is not possible to visit Los Angeles without marveling at the number of automobiles and endless miles of asphalt. However, I always feel quite grateful to be surrounded by so much land

LOS ANGELES
Fresh and Best in Season

Previous page:
I tour Frieda's in Los Angeles.

This page, from top:
With Frieda Caplan, queen of produce.
I join Susan Bowerman and Alex Lombardo.
Interviewing Chef Alex.

producing such an abundance of healthy food. Los Angeles highways lead to the almond, grape, and stone fruit orchards of the Sacramento Valley. The apples of the Sierra Mountains and the mixed orchards of the north and central coasts lie beyond. The vast vegetable fields and fruits of the San Joaquin Valley and the avocado, date, and citrus orchards of southern California beckon.

I feel grateful surrounded by so much land producing such an abundance of healthy food. California farms have led the nation in productivity since 1948. More than half the nation's fresh vegetables are harvested here, and researchers are continuously developing new technology to increase the yield and quality of vegetables, fruits, flowers, and other crops.

Since we didn't have time to set off down the freeway and visit any of these farms firsthand, Susan wisely suggested that we stop in on an old and dear friend who runs a business that would give us a pretty good look at what was growing in fields throughout the world. Frieda's is a distribution center of fresh produce and has become a famous provider of the best in any season from almost any nation. Farmers' markets have been active in California since 1934, the year of my birth, and Frieda Caplan has expanded this local institution to an international level. We found her in a spiffy new location, and I scribbled ideas as we tasted our way through a mountain of perfectly ripe fruits and vegetables.

Having heard so much in the past few years about "California Cuisine," Treena and I were curious to try it on its home turf. We headed north to Santa Monica for lunch with chef Alex Lombardo and brilliant baker Kelly Layne, who share my belief in using the foods that are in season whenever possible. When large quantities of an in-season crop are sent to market, the prices tend to fall and the quality is usually very good. These are often "foods of the people" and you'll find them in any traditional regional cooking. California cooks are very lucky in this respect, having an abundance of agricultural crops and a long growing season in which to take advantage of them. Many people believe that California shapes the way we eat in America. If this is true, I hope we will follow the example of Alice Waters of Chez Panisse in Berkeley and like-minded chefs who are committed to working with local farmers and using high-quality, regional foods.

More and more innovative cooks are taking these basic fresh ingredients and using them in imaginative ways. The ethnic diversity of southern California's population provides a wealth of cooking styles from which to borrow techniques and seasonings, resulting in an exciting mix of styles and flavors.

On our way back to Los Angeles, Susan told me about a new health initiative called the Healthy California 2000 Project, which aims to reduce incidence of coronary heart disease to no more than one hundred cases per hundred thousand people by the year 2000. I have great confidence that they will reach their goal, given a climate suited to year-round exercise and an abundance of healthy food, both in the markets and in restaurants.

Reflecting on our California visit and the wonderful food we enjoyed there, it occurred to me that the key to reducing the amount of calories and excessive fats we consume lies in using "TACT"—taste, aroma, color, and texture. In creating this

The ethnic diversity of southern California's population provides a wealth of cooking styles from which to borrow techniques and seasonings...

Los Angeles menu, I have chosen foods that are naturally endowed with these elements, beginning with a pale, golden Corn Chowder. It is followed by Duck Breasts in Plum Sauce, served with a Celery Root and Potato Purée and a typical California Mesclun Salad. For dessert I have developed an Orange Chocolate Yogurt Cake with help from both Kelly Layne, the California baking wizard we met on our trip, and my pal Susan Purdy, author of *Have Your Cake and Eat It, Too*, which remains a constant source of inspiration to me.

The entire menu with the duck as a main course comes very close to our 1000-calorie target with 18 grams of fat [17% of calories from fat]. For the vegetarian option, I replaced the duck with a roasted winter squash, which brings the total fat grams and calories down quite considerably.

This page, from top:
Kelly Layne concentrates on her baking craft.

Her mouthwatering artistry.

We test dealcoholized Ariel vintages with our winemaker friend Barry Gnekow.

• Cutting Corn

First, trim the stalk end of an ear of corn to make a flat base so that the cob will hold steady. Slice from the top to the bottom, holding a sharp knife parallel to the cob. You don't want to cut too deep or not deep enough—too deep and you will cut off woody pieces of the cob, not deep enough and you will miss out on the sweet white juices of the kernels.

• Soy Milk

I use soy milk to give a smooth and velvety texture to this soup and to the Orange Sauce that accompanies the cake at the end of this section. As I learn more about the health benefits of soy products, I try to use them wherever I can.

Corn Chowder

The moment fresh corn appears at your supermarket or favorite roadside stand, you must rush home and make this delicious golden chowder! Its delicate sweetness is enhanced by a hint of white wine and the smoky saltiness of Canadian bacon.

SERVES 6

- 1/2 teaspoon light olive oil
- 2 cups finely chopped onion
- 6 fresh ears corn, kernels shaved off the cob° [about 3 1/2 cups]
- 1/2 teaspoon dried thyme
- 1 teaspoon finely diced parsley stalks
- 1/4 teaspoon salt
- 1/8 teaspoon freshly ground black pepper
- 1 can [12 fluid ounces or 354 ml] evaporated skim milk
- 2 cups soy milk°
- 2 tablespoons cornstarch
- 4 tablespoons dry white wine [I prefer dealcoholized chardonnay]

Garnish
- 1/3 cup finely diced Canadian bacon
- 1/3 cup finely diced red bell pepper
- 1 tablespoon chopped parsley

1. Warm the oil in a large saucepan over medium-low heat. Sauté the onion and 1/2 cup of the corn kernels until very soft, 12 to 15 minutes. Stir occasionally so the onion doesn't brown. Add the thyme, parsley stalks, salt, and pepper.

2. Transfer the onion mixture to a blender and add 1/2 cup of the evaporated milk. Purée the mixture for about 2 minutes. Add the remaining evaporated milk and blend for another 3 minutes, or until silky smooth. Return to the saucepan along with the remaining corn.

3. Rinse the blender with the soy milk to pick up any flavorful bits

left behind and add to the saucepan with the corn. Bring to a boil, then reduce the heat and simmer for 10 minutes.

4. Combine the cornstarch with the wine to make a slurry. Remove the soup from the heat and stir in the slurry. If you will not be serving the soup right away, set it aside and allow to cool. A few minutes before you are ready to serve, return the soup to the heat and stir occasionally until warm and slightly thickened.

5. To prepare the garnish, warm a small frying pan over medium-high heat. Sauté the Canadian bacon, pepper, and parsley for 3 minutes. [Vegetarian Option: Omit the Canadian bacon.] Remove from the heat and set aside.

6. Serve the chowder in warmed bowls and top each bowl with 1 heaping tablespoon of the Canadian bacon mixture.

Time Estimate
Hands-on, 30 minutes; unsupervised, 10 minutes.

Nutritional Profile per Serving
213 calories; 3 g fat; 0 g saturated fat; 10% of calories from fat; 40 g carbohydrate; 3 g dietary fiber.

Vegetarian Option
Omit the Canadian bacon from the sautéed garnish.

Vegetarian Option Nutritional Profile per Serving
205 calories; 2 g fat; 0 g saturated fat; 9% of calories from fat; 40 g carbohydrate; 3 g dietary fiber.

Portability
Cook the soup through Step 4 and allow to cool. Transport in a container with a tight-fitting lid. Prepare the garnish and carry in a resealable bag. All you will have to do at the party is heat the soup and the garnish and serve.

Duck Breasts in Plum Sauce

• Duck Breasts

This recipe calls for breast meat, so
if you are starting with whole
ducks, you will need to remove the
breasts. Using a sharp knife, cut off
the drumsticks. With the duck
breast-down on the cutting surface,
remove the wings, being careful to
preserve as much breast meat as
possible. Turn the duck over and
make a straight cut just through the
skin and down the center between
the two breasts. Gently cut the meat
away from the breast bones and the
ribs, using the tip of the knife and
lifting the meat away from the bones
with your fingers.

If you are interested in obtaining
frozen, boneless duck breasts, call
D'Artagna, Inc., purveyors of fresh
game and other specialty foods:
[800] 327-8246.

*Happily for those of us who want to limit our fat intake, we can still
enjoy the rich flavor of duck, provided the skin is removed before
serving. The Plum Sauce combines with a wine and orange marinade
to lend an extraordinary balance to the duck. Perhaps we should call
this dish Well-Balanced Duck. You'll notice that I use a flavor injector
for marinating meat; if you don't have one of these handy contraptions,
you'll need to allow an extra eight hours to marinate your duck. Celery
Root and Potato Purée [page 102] and Mesclun Salad with Fruit
[page 103] make elegant companions for this special duck.*

SERVES 6

6 boned duck breast* or 3 whole ducks,
about 4 pounds [1.8 kg] each

Marinade
1/2 teaspoon light olive oil
3 cloves garlic, peeled, bashed, and chopped
1/2 cup dry white wine [I prefer dealcoholized chardonnay]
1/2 cup fresh orange juice
1/8 teaspoon salt
1/8 teaspoon freshly ground black pepper

Plum Sauce
1/2 teaspoon light olive oil
3/4 cup sliced onion
6 red plums, quartered and pitted
1 teaspoon dried oregano
1/3 cup dry red wine
[I prefer dealcoholized cabernet sauvignon]
1 tablespoon brown sugar
1/2 cup fresh orange juice

Vegetarian Option [per Serving]
1/2 acorn or delicata squash, seeds and pulp removed
1/4 cup cooked garbanzo beans
1 teaspoon freshly grated Parmesan cheese
1/2 orange, sectioned

1 red plum, peeled, seeded, and sliced into wedges
1 green onion, trimmed and cut into thin
   lengthwise strips
   Sliced cilantro leaves

To Prepare the Duck

1. If you are starting with whole ducks, see sidebar for carving instructions.

2. Lay the duck breasts skin side down in a glass baking dish.

To Prepare the Marinade

3. Warm the oil in a small saucepan over medium heat. Sauté the garlic for 1 minute, then stir in the white wine, orange juice, salt, and pepper. Bring the mixture to a boil, then reduce the heat and simmer very gently for 20 minutes.

4. Strain the marinade through a sieve into a measuring cup and pour into a flavor injector.* Inject as much marinade as possible into each breast. Set aside any leftover marinade to use in the sauce. If you don't have a flavor injector, pour the marinade over the breasts, cover, and refrigerate for at least 8 hours.

To Prepare the Sauce

5. Warm the oil in a large saucepan over medium-high heat. Sauté the onion until transparent, soft, and lightly browned, about 6 minutes. Add the plums, oregano, red wine, and sugar. Cover and bring to a boil, then reduce the heat and simmer for 25 minutes.

6. Strain the sauce through a sieve set over a saucepan, discarding the pulp. Stir in the orange juice and set the sauce aside. [Vegetarian Option: Set aside 1/4 cup of sauce per vegetarian serving before proceeding to next step.]

To Cook the Duck Breasts

7. Heat a large frying pan over medium-high heat. Dry the breasts and lay them in the pan, skin side down. [The reason I leave the skin on the breasts is to preserve moisture and make the meat more tender. All the fat will be drained before

*Flavor Injector

When you remove fat, you must replace it with more flavor and aroma. This device, an oversized plastic syringe, is filled with a marinade or infusion, which is then injected into meat or fruit. I have found this method to be much more effective than a traditional marinade, which barely permeates the surface.

serving.] Sprinkle the meat with salt and pepper. Brown for about 2 minutes to render some of the fat into the pan. Turn the breasts and seal the flesh side for another 2 minutes. Turn back onto the skin side for 4 minutes.

8. Transfer the breasts to a plate and remove the skin, being careful to reserve any juices that drain onto the plate. Return the breasts to the frying pan and lightly brown the skinned side, then remove to a warmed plate and cover to keep warm.

9. Pour the fat out of the frying pan, but do not clean it. Add any remaining marinade to the pan along with the reserved duck juices and bring to a boil, scraping the flavorful bits from the bottom with a spurtle or wooden spoon. Remove from the heat and strain through a sieve into the saucepan with the plum sauce. Stir to combine, then pour the sauce into the large frying pan.

10. Add the duck breasts to the sauce and warm over medium heat. Remove the breasts as soon as they are heated through and carve in thin diagonal slices across the grain.

To Serve

11. Spoon a puddle of hot plum sauce onto a warmed dinner plate and arrange a few slices of duck breast on top of the sauce. Place a scoop of Celery Root and Potato Purée and a serving of Mesclun Salad with Fruit alongside.

Time Estimate
Hands-on, 45 minutes; unsupervised, 25 minutes.

Nutritional Profile per Serving
263 calories; 11 g fat; 4 g saturated fat; 37% of calories from fat; 20 g carbohydrate; 2 g dietary fiber.

Vegetarian Option: Acorn Squash with Citrus and Garbanzos
Season the squash with salt and pepper and bake skin side up in a roasting pan at 350 degrees F [180 degrees C] for 25 minutes, or until tender. Pour the 1/4 cup of reserved sauce into the well in the

center of the squash, top with the garbanzo beans and Parmesan cheese, and heat in the oven for 5 minutes. Remove from the oven and fill the squash with orange sections and plum slices combined with a few strips of onion and sliced cilantro leaves.

Vegetarian Option Nutritional Profile per Serving
178 calories; 3 g fat; 0 g saturated fat; 12% of calories from fat; 40 g carbohydrate; 5 g dietary fiber.

Celery Root and Potato Purée

Mashed potatoes are one of the best comfort foods I know, even without a pat of butter melting on top. This dish is the Rolls Royce of mashed potatoes, all dressed up with puréed celery root, or celeriac as it is sometimes called. The celery root gives this humble dish an extra level of flavor and consistency, not to mention nutrition.

SERVES 6

1	celery root* [about 1 pound or 450 g]
2	large russet potatoes
1/4	teaspoon salt
1/4	cup yogurt cheese [page 37]
1/4	teaspoon white pepper
3	tablespoons finely sliced fresh celery leaves

1. Scrub the celery root with a vegetable brush. Cut off the top and bottom and discard. Peel the celery root with a knife, making sure to cut out all the brown spots and any woody parts near the center. Slice thickly and then cut into 1-inch [2½-cm] pieces.

2. Peel the potatoes and cut into 1-inch [2½-cm] slices. Put the celery root, potatoes, salt, and 2 cups of water into a medium saucepan. Cover and bring to a boil, then simmer for 25 minutes, or until very soft.

3. Strain the vegetables and mash well. Stir in the yogurt cheese, white pepper, and sliced celery leaves. Cover until ready to serve.

Time Estimate
Hands-on, 15 minutes; unsupervised, 25 minutes.

Nutritional Profile per Serving
155 calories; 0 g fat; 0 g saturated fat; 1% of calories from fat; 35 g carbohydrate; 3 g dietary fiber.

*Celeriac
Pronounced "seh-LER-ee-ak," this brown, knobby root mass has a wonderful flavor that is a combination of celery and parsley. Also called celery root, it is available from fall to spring. Choose smooth, firm roots that weigh less than a pound. If wrapped in plastic and refrigerated, they should keep a week or more. Celeriac is very popular in Europe where it is often used in marinated salads and puréed soups. To use, remove the stalks and scrub the root with a vegetable brush. Cut off any protruding knobs and peel the root with a vegetable peeler or paring knife.

Mesclun Salad with Fruit

Mesclun, a mixture of interesting greens, usually includes wonderful salad greens like arugula, chickweed and radicchio, depending on what's fresh and in season. I'm pleased to see it appearing in so many supermarkets around the United States. Experiment with what you find in your supermarket and don't hesitate to ask your produce manager to special order.

SERVES 6

Dressing

- 1/2 teaspoon arrowroot
- 1/4 cup dry white wine [I prefer dealcoholized chardonnay]
- 1/4 cup fresh orange juice
- 1 teaspoon rice wine vinegar

Salad

- 3 oranges, peeled and segmented, reserving any juice for the dressing
- 6 plums, quartered, pitted, and sliced
- 1/4 cup thinly sliced red onion
- 3 tablespoons slivered cilantro
- 3 cups mesclun [mixed salad greens]

To Prepare the Dressing

1. Combine the arrowroot with the wine in a small saucepan and stir over medium heat until clear and slightly thickened. Stir in the orange juice and vinegar. Set aside to cool.

To Prepare the Salad

2. Place the oranges, plums, onion, and cilantro in a large salad bowl. When the dressing has cooled, pour it over the fruit and toss to mix well. Set aside until ready to serve.

3. To serve, toss mixed greens and dressed fruit.

Time Estimate
Hands-on, 25 minutes.

Nutritional Profile per Serving
68 calories; o g fat; o g saturated fat; 3% of calories from fat;
17 g carbohydrate; 6 g dietary fiber.

Orange Chocolate Yogurt Cake

My culinary colleague Suzanne Thostenson and I have worked hard to perfect the art of baking low-fat cakes, still a very pleasing dessert to many of us. This delicacy is the perfect end to this elegant California menu and would be equally as impressive for a birthday. And, with only four grams of fat and all that flavor, anyone can enjoy it!

SERVES 6

*Cake flour

Milled from soft wheat, cake flour has less gluten than other flours, which helps keep low-fat baked goods more tender.

- 1/3 cup Dutch-process or European-style cocoa
- 1/2 cup firmly packed brown sugar
- 1/4 cup boiling water
- 1/2 cup plain nonfat yogurt
- 1 1/2 tablespoons light olive oil
- 1 1/2 tablespoons corn syrup
- 1 1/2 tablespoons unsweetened applesauce
- 1 large egg yolk
- 1 1/2 teaspoons vanilla extract
- 1 teaspoon grated orange zest [optional]
- 3/4 cup unsifted cake flour*
- 1 tablespoon cornstarch
- 1 teaspoon baking powder
- 1/2 teaspoon baking soda
- Pinch of salt
- 2 large egg whites, at room temperature
- 2 tablespoons granulated sugar

Orange Sauce
- 1 cup yogurt cheese [page 37]
- 1/4 cup 1% soy milk or skim milk
- 1/4 cup frozen orange juice concentrate
- 2 tablespoons pure maple syrup
- 1 teaspoon grated orange zest
- 1 teaspoon fresh lemon juice

Garnish
- 2 oranges, peeled and segmented [18 segments]
- 6 mint sprigs

To Prepare the Cake

1. Preheat the oven to 350 degrees F [180 degrees C]. Make sure the egg whites are at room temperature before beginning the recipe.

2. Spray an 8-inch [20-cm] round cake pan with cooking spray. Cut a round of parchment or waxed paper to fit the bottom of the pan. Smooth the paper into the pan, spray with cooking spray, and coat the bottom and sides with flour. Set aside.

3. Combine the cocoa and brown sugar in a small bowl. Pour in the boiling water and stir until smooth. Set aside to cool.

4. In a large bowl, whisk together the yogurt, oil, corn syrup, applesauce, egg yolk, vanilla, and orange zest. Add the chocolate mixture and mix thoroughly.

5. In a separate bowl, combine the cake flour, cornstarch, baking powder, soda, and salt. Stir the dry ingredients gently into the chocolate mixture.

6. Make sure the bowl and whip attachment of your electric mixer are perfectly clean and grease-free. Beat the egg whites until soft peaks form. Sprinkle the sugar slowly over the top, one tablespoon at a time, and continue to beat until the whites are stiff but not dry.

7. Stir a large spoonful of beaten egg whites into the batter to lighten it. Gently fold in the rest of the egg whites in two steps.

8. Pour the batter into the prepared pan and bake for 35 to 40 minutes, or until a toothpick or cake tester inserted in the center comes out clean. Cool on a rack for twenty minutes, then tip out of the pan onto another rack to cool completely. The cake will fall slightly as it cools. This cake is best served the same day it is baked, but if you allow it to cool completely and then wrap it carefully, it will be fine the next day.

To Prepare the Sauce

9. In a medium bowl, whisk together the yogurt cheese, milk, orange juice concentrate, syrup, orange zest, and lemon juice.

Keep whisking until the sauce is perfectly smooth. This sauce can be made ahead and refrigerated.

To Serve

10. Cut the cake into eight wedges. Place a wedge on each dessert plate and top with a spoonful of sauce. Lay a few orange segments and a sprig of mint on the side. [Leftover cake will keep for a few days if wrapped in plastic.]

Time Estimate

Hands-on, 30 minutes; unsupervised, 2 hours.

Nutritional Profile per Serving

276 calories; 4 g fat; 1 g saturated fat; 13% of calories from fat; 52 g carbohydrate; 4 g dietary fiber.

Portability

The cake can be returned to its baking pan after it has cooled or placed on a plate and covered to take to the party. The yogurt sauce can go back into the yogurt container or other plastic container. Cut the orange segments at home and carry them in a plastic container along with the mint sprigs.

soup
Watercress Soup
Beautiful bright green soup enlivened with chili powder and pinto beans.

main course
Ensenada Seafood Stew with Roasted Tomato Salsa
Rich in seafood and vegetables with the creamy finish of yogurt sauce.

vegetarian option
Hearts of Artichoke and Palm

side dish
Saffron Rice
Beautiful amber grains with a hint of saffron.

dessert
Sweet Potato Mousse
Creamy textures combine with raisins, brown sugar, and orange zest.

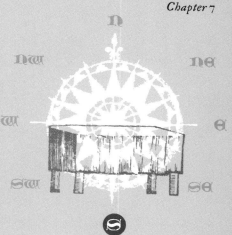

travelogue

You might wonder what Treena and I were doing looping back to Mexico after our stop in Los Angeles. Our return to Mexico was caused by a quirk of maritime law, and one for which I am quite thankful. You see, the Jones Act states that only vessels registered in the United States can carry passengers to more than two consecutive U.S. ports. That meant that the QE II, which is registered in the United Kingdom, had already visited Los Angeles and now had to backtrack to Mexico before setting out across the Pacific for two more U.S. ports in Hawaii. What a joy, the Jones Act!

So it was that we found ourselves sailing into a crescent-shaped bay in northern Baja. The Baja is a long peninsula cut off from mainland Mexico by a deep, narrow body of water called either the Sea of Cortez or the Gulf of California, depending on the map you use.

Ensenada, often called the "Cinderella of the Pacific," is the third largest city on the peninsula. Its closeness to California is a big attraction to tourists in search of something different.

ENSENADA
Bounty from Earth and Sea

Cortez arrived in Baja in 1533, busily looking for the pearls he had heard were abundant along the Pacific. He recorded the presence of three Indian tribes on the peninsula; the northernmost group he called the Cochimies. These tribes soon found themselves sharing their homeland with occasional pirates laying in wait for Spanish ships sailing between Acapulco and the northwest coast of the Philippines. Catholic priests built a series of missions along the peninsula in the 1700s, and the Spanish militia came and went, but

Synergy of sea, desert, and the isolated Baja history created a unique cuisine.

the desert climate was not conducive to agriculture or large settlements, and the area remained in relative isolation. At the time of Mexico's emancipation in 1821, the Indian population had been reduced to about four thousand people. Only about a thousand Cochimies survive today, and thanks to the help of a kind anthropologist we met, we were able to visit with a member of the tribe. She graciously shared a meal of watercress soup, one of the dishes passed down from her pre-Hispanic ancestors.

Previous page:
Ensenada's fish market is spotless, and our guide is an expert.
This seafood mix promises it is "excellent food if you are feeling tired."

This page, from top:
The hustle and bustle of the Ensenada market is enticing.
Interviewing on location at an organic farm.

As we drove back to Ensenada, I was thinking of the creativity and resourcefulness these people drew upon to survive the harsh desert climate and the isolation of an island-like environment, not to mention the harsh blows dealt by the history of the last four centuries. Even after its emancipation from Spain, Mexico's well-documented struggle with the United States harmed a great many people. It is surprising, therefore, that Americans don't find an undercurrent of hostility when visiting Baja. On the contrary, everyone we met welcomed us with warmth, hospitality, and generosity.

During our visit, Treena and I visited with farmers, home cooks, restaurant chefs, and purveyors of fresh produce and fish. We were entranced by a visit to Ensenada's famous fish market, spotlessly clean and full of every sort of seafood, plus kiosks selling tamales and tacos by the thousands. We were told by one vendor that a jumble of seafood, celery, carrots and onions was "excellent food if you are feeling tired"—very good advice, indeed.

One of our most memorable Ensenada meals took place in the picturesque La Embotelldora Vieja [The Old Bottling Plant], a converted wine cellar that is now an extremely elegant, cool respite from the sun. We sampled food from a number of local restaurants, spread on a buffet table surrounded by huge thirty-foot wine casks, still in use today. More than ninety percent of the wine produced in Mexico comes from the Santa Tomas valley outside Ensenada, where a cold marine current produces just the right microclimate for growing grapes. The people here are very proud of the quality of the wines and excited about the prospects for other types of agriculture in this area because of the development of deep-well irrigation. Everyone I talked to in Ensenada was full of an infectious enthusiasm and hope for the future. The new technology to make desert land productive, combined with the abundant seafood from the Pacific, make for exciting possibilities, and I left with the feeling that something extraordinary was about to happen to these resourceful people.

Just one small note of concern: Coastal fishing industries all around the world are facing potential disaster. If we don't somehow manage to bring effective, international controls to our waters, we will eventually run out of this extremely healthy food supply. If you see or hear of a group that is trying to bring sanity to the sea, get involved. In the meantime, use smaller portions. More than six ounces at one sitting is simply too much for both us and our world. If you're interested in learning more about this, look up this site on the internet: http: www.sacbee.com.

In sorting through my notes and memories from our Ensenada visit, I was struck with how the synergy of sea, desert, and the isolated history of the Baja created a unique cuisine. It was the time we spent with a member of the Cochimi tribe that most influenced the menu I have developed for you and your guests, and it is a privilege to be able to share their watercress soup with others. For our main course, I experimented with the clam and seafood chowder we enjoyed in Ensenada and brought it together in a roasted tomato seafood stew that is served with a bright saffron rice, reminiscent of its Spanish roots. Finally, we tip our hats to the local sweet potato with a delicious mousse.

All of this is possible for just over 900 calories and 8 grams of fat, for a healthy 8% of calories from fat. The entire meal is chock full of good flavor, satisfying textures, and wonderful aromas. Isn't this just what we're looking for on the lighter side?

This page, from top:
Getting to know new friends in "The Old Bottling Plant."

The day included a splendid buffet of local specialties.

An anthropoligist friend shows us a Cochimi basket used to preserve food.

Watercress Soup

Thanks to the hospitality of the people of the Cochimi tribe of Northern Baja, we were able to taste their original watercress "soup," which is much like a warm, wilted salad. I've made a few minor changes, but this still provides a delicious insight into a very special people's way of life and health.

SERVES 6

*Summer Savory

This is not a typical Mexican herb, but I think it is a wonderful companion to beans and perks up our watercress soup beautifully. You may find it fresh in markets or produce sections, and it's an easy garden herb to grow from seed, too.

- 1/2 teaspoon light olive oil
- 2 cups finely chopped onion
- 1/2 teaspoon ground cumin
- 1 teaspoon dried summer savory*
- 1/4 teaspoon salt
- 2 cans pinto beans [15 1/2 ounces or 434 g each], rinsed and drained
- 3 1/2 cups low-sodium chicken or vegetable stock
- 4 cups roughly chopped watercress, carefully washed and stemmed
- 1 tablespoon fresh lemon juice
- 1 1/4 teaspoons mild chili powder
- 6 corn tortillas

Garnish

- 6 tablespoons finely sliced watercress stalks
- 6 sprigs watercress, about 6 inches long

1. Warm the oil in a large saucepan over medium heat. Sauté the onions until translucent and soft, about 5 minutes. Stir in the cumin, summer savory, salt, and pinto beans. Cook for an additional 3 minutes.

2. Bring the stock to a boil in a medium saucepan. [Vegetarian Option: Use vegetable stock.] Stir in the watercress and cook for 3 minutes. Add the stock and greens to the bean mixture and stir to incorporate.

3. Process 2 cups of the soup in a blender until no whole beans remain, about 1 minute. Return the purée to the saucepan, stir

in the lemon juice and chili powder, and bring to a boil. Cover
and keep warm until ready to serve.

4. Wrap the tortillas in waxed paper and cook for 2 minutes at
High in a microwave oven. Or wrap in aluminum foil and heat
in the oven for 10 minutes at 350 degrees F [180 degrees C].

5. To serve, spoon a portion of soup into a warmed soup bowl and
top with the diced watercress stems. Roll a nice stalk of
watercress in a warm tortilla and serve alongside.

Time Estimate
Hands-on, 25 minutes.

Nutritional Profile per Serving
226 calories; 2 g fat; 0 g saturated fat; 9% of calories from fat;
42 g carbohydrate; 10 g dietary fiber.

Portability
The soup can be prepared ahead and carried in a container with a
tight lid. Carry the watercress garnishes in a resealable bag, and
either wrap the tortillas in foil or carry them in their original bag.

Ensenada Seafood Stew
with Roasted Tomato Salsa

I hope you'll appreciate the health-giving properties of this stew and find, as our vendor advised, that it relieves you from "feeling tired." I have added to this traditional stew a creamy finish that distinguished a fine soup I was served in our wine-cask restaurant. In essence, it may remind you of a creamy version of a paella. Serve this with a mound of Saffron Rice [page 119] and a bit of Roasted Tomato Salsa [page 118].

SERVES 6

Stew

8	ounces [227 g] squid "steaks," free of cartilage and tentacles
12	small clams in the shell
12	ounces [340 g] large prawns
6	ounces [170 g] orange roughy fillet
2	teaspoons light olive oil
1	large sweet onion, roughly chopped
3	cloves garlic, peeled, bashed, and chopped
3	carrots, peeled and cut on the diagonal into $^1/_4$-inch [$^3/_4$-cm] slices [1 cup]
3	stalks celery, cut on the diagonal into $^1/_2$-inch [$1^1/_2$-cm] slices [1 cup]
1	red bell pepper, cored and cut into 1-inch [$2^1/_2$-cm] strips
1	cup quartered mushrooms
$^1/_2$	cup dry white wine [I prefer dealcoholized chardonnay]
$^1/_2$	cup low-sodium fish or vegetable stock
$^1/_4$	teaspoon salt
$^1/_4$	teaspoon freshly ground black pepper

Sauce

1	cup yogurt cheese [page 37]
$^1/_4$	cup arrowroot
$^1/_2$	cup dry white wine [I prefer dealcoholized chardonnay]
2	cups low-sodium fish or vegetable stock

3 tablespoons Roasted Tomato Salsa [page 118], or
to taste

Garnish

1/4 cup chopped cilantro

Vegetarian Option

2 small cooked artichoke hearts, fresh or canned, cut
in half

2 canned hearts of palm, cut diagonally into 3 pieces

To Prepare the Stew

1. Cut the squid into 1-inch [2½-cm] squares. Cover with water in
a small saucepan and cook over low heat for 25 minutes. If the
squid has been tenderized [it will be full of tiny holes made by
tenderizing needles], it will cook tender in about 5 minutes.
Strain and place the chopped squid in a pile on a large plate.

2. Scrub the clams and place in a frying pan with 1/4 cup water.
Cover and bring to a boil. Remove from the heat as soon as the
clams open, 3 to 5 minutes. When cool enough to handle,
remove the meat from the shells. Place the clams in a separate
pile on the plate with the squid.

3. Peel the prawns, leaving on the last bit of shell and the tail. If
they haven't been previously deveined, make a shallow cut
down the back of each prawn and remove the gritty digestive
tract. Place the prawns on the plate with the squid and clams.

4. Cut the orange roughy fillet into 1-inch [2½-cm] squares. Add
to the plate with the other fish, cover, and refrigerate until
ready to cook.

5. Warm 1 teaspoon of the oil in a large high-sided skillet over
medium-high heat. Sauté the onion for 2 minutes to release its
flavorful oils. Toss in the garlic and cook for 1 more minute.
Add the carrots, celery, pepper, and mushrooms. Stir for a
minute or two, then add the wine.

6. Boil, uncovered, over medium-high heat until the carrots are
tender, 10 to 12 minutes. Add up to 1/2 cup of the fish or

vegetable stock as the liquid evaporates. [Vegetarian Option: Use vegetable stock here. Set aside $1/6$ of this mixture for each vegetarian serving before proceeding to the next step.]

7. Heat the remaining 1 teaspoon of oil in a large saucepan or small Dutch oven. Add the prawns and orange roughy, sprinkle with the salt and pepper, and cook for 30 seconds. Gently stir in the cooked vegetables, clams, and squid. Remove from the heat while you prepare the sauce.

To Prepare the Sauce

8. Spoon the yogurt cheese into a 4-cup glass measure.

9. Mix the arrowroot with the wine to make a slurry. Combine the stock and the slurry in a saucepan and stir over medium heat until thick and glossy. [Vegetarian Option: Use vegetable stock here. Set aside $1/4$ cup of sauce at the end of this step.] Pour a little of the hot, thickened stock into the yogurt cheese and mix well to temper the yogurt. Add the rest of the stock to the yogurt cheese and whisk until no pure white remains.

10. Pour the sauce over the fish and vegetables. Add salsa to your taste and heat very gently, not allowing the stew to boil.

To Serve

11. Place a scoop of saffron rice in the center of a warmed dinner plate and surround the rice with a ring of stew. Garnish with the chopped cilantro and pass the remaining salsa for those, like Treena, who like it hot.

Time Estimate
Hands-on, 1 hour; unsupervised, 25 minutes.

Nutritional Profile per Serving
289 calories; 4 g fat; 1 g saturated fat; 13% of calories from fat; 30 g carbohydrate; 3 g dietary fiber.

Vegetarian Option: Hearts of Artichoke and Palm
When almost ready to serve, heat the reserved vegetable mixture in a small saucepan. Add the artichoke hearts and hearts of palm

and heat through. Pour the reserved yogurt cheese sauce over the heated vegetables and season with salsa to taste. Heat very gently, not allowing it to boil.

Vegetarian Option Nutritional Profile per Serving
287 calories; 4 g fat; o g saturated fat; 10% of calories from fat; 57 g carbohydrate; 5 g dietary fiber.

Roasted Tomato Salsa

I'm very grateful to the excellent "Rick Bayless's Mexican Kitchen," for this perfectly flavored tomato salsa. It's hot!

- 1 pound [450 g] Italian plum tomatoes, such as Roma
- 2 fresh jalapeño peppers*
- 3 cloves garlic, unpeeled
- 1/2 teaspoon salt
- 1/3 cup finely chopped sweet onion
- 1/2 cup loosely packed chopped cilantro

1. Preheat the broiler.
2. Line a shallow baking pan with aluminum foil and lay the whole tomatoes on it. Broil the tomatoes until their skins are blistered and blackened, about 6 minutes. Turn and blacken the other side. Cool and peel, reserving the juices.
3. Heat a heavy frying pan over medium heat. Lay the chiles and garlic in the dry pan and turn occasionally until soft, 5 to 10 minutes for the chiles and up to 15 minutes for the garlic. A quick pinch will tell you if they are ready. They should be softened and yield to slight pressure. Cool, peel the garlic, and remove the stems from the chiles.
4. Pulse the chiles, garlic, and salt in a blender or food processor. Add the tomatoes and their reserved juice and pulse a few times more, until coarsely chopped. Pour the mixture into a bowl, stir in the onion and cilantro, and set aside until ready to serve. This salsa will keep in the refrigerator for one or two days.

Time Estimate
Hands-on, 25 minutes.

Nutritional Profile per Serving
28 calories; 0 g fat; 0 g saturated fat; 0% of calories from fat; 6 g carbohydrate; 1 g dietary fiber.

*Chiles

There are so many wonderful chiles available now in supermarkets and produce departments throughout the U.S. that I urge you to get acquainted with them. This recipe calls for rather hot ones, but there is a great variety. Anaheim chiles are quite versatile, too. You could certainly buy fresh Anaheim chiles and roast them but there are so many great ways to use chiles that I recommend buying diced green chiles in a can. If you choose to roast your own, about a pound of chiles will produce an ounce of roasted, peeled chiles.

Saffron Rice

This is a fine, fragrant rice that I can imagine working in a number of different menus. Perhaps it will become a signature dish for you.

SERVES 6

<blockquote>

1/2 teaspoon light olive oil

3/4 cup chopped onion

1 cup long-grain white rice

13/4 cups low-sodium fish or vegetable stock

1/4 teaspoon salt

1 pinch of powdered saffron [*page 24*]

</blockquote>

1. Warm the oil in a saucepan over medium-high heat. Sauté the onion until translucent, 2 or 3 minutes. Add the rice and cook until it turns chalky white, another 2 or 3 minutes.

2. Pour in the stock and season with the salt and saffron. [Vegetarian Option: Use vegetable stock.] Cover, bring to a boil, then reduce the heat as low as possible. Cook for 20 minutes, remove from the heat, and set aside for 5 minutes before serving.

Time Estimate
Hands-on, 10 minutes; unsupervised, 25 minutes.

Nutritional Profile per Serving
157 calories; 1 g fat; 0 g saturated fat; 4% of calories from fat; 33 g carbohydrate; 1 g dietary fiber.

Sweet Potato Mousse

*The sweet potato is one of the Americas' greatest gifts to the world.
Nutritious, delicious—surely it is the king, or perhaps queen, of all root
vegetables. I concocted this combination of oranges, raisins, and allspice
to complement, but not mask, its creamy sweetness. The result is akin to
a delicately textured mousse packed with interesting tastes.*

SERVES 6

1/2	cup fresh orange juice
1/3	cup raisins
3	tablespoons brown sugar
3/8	teaspoon ground allspice
3	pounds sweet potatoes, peeled and roughly chopped
1/8	teaspoon salt
1/2	cup yogurt cheese [page 37]
1/2	teaspoon freshly grated orange zest
1	tablespoon slivered almonds

Garnish

Edible flowers such as pansies, nasturtiums, or
bachelor buttons.

1. Preheat the oven to 400 degrees F [205 degrees C].

2. Warm the orange juice in a small saucepan over medium heat.
   Add the raisins, 2 tablespoons of the brown sugar, and
   1/8 teaspoon of the allspice to the warm juice. Set aside and let
   the raisins soak while the potatoes are cooking.

3. Put the potatoes and salt in a large saucepan, cover with water,
   and bring to a boil. Cook for 15 minutes, or until very soft.
   Drain the cooking liquid and return the potatoes to the pan.
   Cover the potatoes with a clean dishtowel and place over low
   heat for 5 to 10 minutes, or until the potatoes have a dry,
   floury appearance.

4. Mash with a potato masher and add the yogurt cheese,
   remaining 1/4 teaspoon of allspice, and orange zest.

5. Drain the raisins and set aside to use for garnish. Add their marinade to the potatoes and stir until smooth.

6. Spray a 10-inch [25-cm] round ovenproof baking dish with cooking spray and spread the potatoes in the dish. Set aside until ready to bake.

7. To bake, texturize the potatoes with the tines of a fork and sprinkle the remaining tablespoon of brown sugar and the almonds over the top. Bake in the preheated oven for 15 minutes.

8. To serve, scoop a portion of the potato mousse onto a dessert plate and top with a few of the plumped raisins. Set an edible flower alongside.

Time Estimate
Hands-on, 25 minutes; unsupervised, 15 minutes.

Nutritional Profile per Serving
231 calories; 1 g fat; 0 g saturated fat; 3% of calories from fat; 52 g carbohydrate; 5 g dietary fiber.

Portability
Prepare the dish through Step 6. Carry the brown sugar and almonds in a resealable bag and sprinkle on just before baking. Put the mousse in the oven as you start the main course so it can be served warm.

dessert 7. ENSENADA

appetizer
Waimea Fried Rice
Risotto-like, spiked with fresh ginger, pineapple, and cilantro.

main course
Roasted Chicken with Pineapple Curry Sauce
Tropical chicken flavored with a curry pineapple-ginger sauce.

vegetarian option
Sautéed Banana with Pineapple Curry Sauce

vegetable
Vegetable Stir-Fry with Passion Fruit Vinaigrette
Great fruit flavors tossed with fine fresh vegetables.

dessert
Lychee Sorbet with Fruit Salsa
Refreshing blend of lychees and gingerroot with a tropical fruit and mint salsa.

travelogue

*O*n our fourth day at sea after leaving Ensenada, Treena and I began scanning the horizon for the first sight of land, and when we spotted the volcanic tip of Mauna Loa and the white peak of Mauna Kea rising from the sea, it felt like a homecoming. Years ago, we were *Kama'ainas* [local residents] on the Big Island, as Hawaii is known. [It is twice as large as all the other major islands combined.] We lived just south of Kailua-Kona for three years or so, and we often think back on those days of sunshine, tropical breezes, and the scent of coffee. Kona means leeward, which also means the dry or sheltered side of an island, and on Hawaii that translates into ideal conditions for raising coffee. The distinctive Kona coffee beans are grown on small farms along the lower slopes of the mountains that run between Mt. Hualalai and Mauna Loa, where they ripen to perfection in the sun.

Leeward also means good place for a port, and as we cruised into the bay at Kailua-Kona, I was thinking of another group of sailors who moored their boats along this sheltered shore. These were the

KAILUA-KONA
Tropical Tastes in a Garden Paradise

ancient Polynesian mariners who first colonized these islands, and I have often wondered how they must have felt when they spotted the distant humps that became their new home. Anthropologists believe that these original Hawaiians came from the Marquesas, a group of islands over two thousand miles south. They set out on the open sea in large canoes filled with pots of taro, sugarcane, ginger, sweet potatoes and even arrowroot! They also brought dogs, pigs, fowl, and possibly a few stowaway rats. No one knows on which island they made landfall about 400 A.D., but all the larger islands were inhabited when Captain Cook arrived in 1778. He was astonished to discover that the islanders spoke the same language

Relics of ancient civilization can still be found in the form of *heiaus* and *petroglyphs*.

as tribes he had visited in the South Pacific, and the Hawaiians were equally amazed at the size of their visitor's canoe. Although Cook was killed in a skirmish on Hawaii the following year, his arrival signaled the beginning of foreign influence on the islands and the dilution of the native culture. Relics of the ancient civilization that flourished here can still be found on the Big Island in the form of *heiaus* [old temple sites] and petroglyphs carved into lava rock.

Our visit, however, was more about food than history, and Treena and I were keen to find chefs who were using traditional foods in innovative ways. We were escorted on our search by Jean Hull, the energetic director of the University of Hawaii's outstation at Kealakekua. Jean is a registered dietitian, chef instructor, and dedicated promoter of local foods and local people. Part of her work is to conduct the American Culinary Federation's nutrition education for professional chefs.

Jean took us out to the town of Waimea on the northern part of the island to visit some of her former students who were cooking at the legendary Merriman's Restaurant. Waimea is quite rural and, being on the windward side of the island, is a lovely spot to visit when you tire of the humid summer heat on the sheltered Kona coast. The grass is green, the trees are lush, the flowers are brilliant against a white picket fence, and Peter Merriman's small, elegant restaurant is perched invitingly in the sun.

I was extremely impressed with Peter's intriguing use of what I call those foods that are fresh and best in season. He is an innovator, yet he resists changes that may adversely affect the environment, especially the sea. Local fish are being rapidly depleted, and Peter serves four-ounce portions of seafood because, as he explains, "someone has to start somewhere to stop the overconsumption that threatens several entire species." I like Peter's passion and his purpose. We could learn something from the ancient Hawaiians, who would periodically declare certain fishing grounds *kapu* [taboo] so they could revitalize.

Although sugarcane and pineapple are still the island's main products, over two hundred and fifty other crops are now grown commercially here. The island's diverse topography makes itpossible to raise a wide range of fruits and vegetables. Papayas thrive in the rocky lava fields, while onions and vegetables prefer the rich volcanic soils. Cool season crops such as cabbages and strawberries grow in the higher elevations of windward slopes, leaving the lowlands for tropical fruits like bananas, mangoes, and lychees.

Peter Merriman's style had a great deal of influence on this Big Island dinner, which has pineapple as its theme song. Many people think, and understandably so, that pineapples are native to Hawaii, but they are not. No one is sure exactly how the fruit arrived on the island, but one theory is that they floated ashore from a wrecked Spanish ship during the early days of Pacific sea traffic. The first white settlers found these juicy bromeliads growing wild on the islands, and by the 1850s they were being planted as a commercial crop.

Now you may think this menu offers an excess of pineapple, but you will find that the fruit sounds a repetitive chord in each course, threading the meal together with a variety of textures like the adagio from Dvorak's Cello Concerto in B Minor. For a prelude

This Big Island dinner has pineapple as its theme song.

we have aromatic fried rice, indicative of the Asian influences on the island. Our main course is an incredible roast chicken in a pineapple-flavored curry sauce. Dessert is a lychee sorbet with a fruit salsa of strawberries, mango, and...pineapple!! This pineapple concerto adds up to less than 800 calories and 13 grams of fat, with even less for the vegetarian option. If you're trying to eat in the 10 to 15% calories-from-fat range, you will be very happy with this island meal.

Waimea Fried Rice

This delicious brown-rice appetizer is full of wonderful aromas from ginger, garlic, and Thai fish sauce. Jalapeño pepper, celery, and lemongrass add texture, while red peppers, golden pineapple, and green cilantro reflect a rainbow of island color. You may encounter a temptation to add more oil; please resist, as it isn't necessary.

SERVES 6

1	cup long-grain brown rice
1	stalk fresh lemongrass
1	tablespoon light oil
1	teaspoon toasted sesame oil
1	jalapeño pepper, cored, seeded, and finely diced [1 tablespoon]
3	cloves garlic, peeled, bashed, and finely chopped
1/3	cup red bell pepper, cut into 1/4-inch [3/4-cm] dice
1/2	cup celery, cut into 1/4-inch [3/4-cm] dice
4	teaspoons grated gingerroot
1	cup chopped fresh pineapple [1/4-inch or 3/4-cm dice]
12	mint leaves, finely chopped
1/4	cup loosely packed cilantro leaves, finely chopped
1	tablespoon Thai fish sauce* or tamari
1	teaspoon rice wine vinegar

Garnish

6	sprigs fresh mint
6	sprigs cilantro

1. In a medium saucepan, boil the rice in 4 cups of water for 25 minutes, or until just tender. Drain through a sieve and rinse with cold water to wash off the starch and cool the rice. Spread the rice in a flat metal pan and refrigerate for at least 30 minutes.

2. This is a dish that cooks quite quickly from this point on, so it's important to have all the ingredients prepared and ready at hand.

•Thai Fish Sauce

Nam pla is as essential to Thai cooking as soy sauce is to Chinese. It is a clear, salty liquid made from salted fermented fish. It is used as an ingredient in many dishes and in dipping sauces. It has a powerful smell but a mellow flavor that seems to enhance other flavors in a dish. It is rich in Vitamin B and will keep indefinitely with very little loss of color or flavor. It can be found in many supermarkets and most Asian groceries.

3. Remove the tough outside layer of the lemongrass and cut off the root end and the dry top. Start slicing from the root end and use only the most tender, bulb-like part of the stalk. Slice thinly and chop very fine so the flavor will be spread throughout. You should have about $1/4$ cup, chopped.

4. Warm the oil in a large frying pan over medium-high heat. Sauté the lemongrass, chiles, and garlic for 30 seconds to release the aromatic oils. Add the red pepper, celery, and ginger and stir-fry for another 30 seconds.

5. Add the chilled rice and cook until heated through, stirring occasionally to keep it from sticking. Add the pineapple, mint, and cilantro to the hot rice. Sprinkle the fish sauce, vinegar, and sesame oil over the top. [Vegetarian Option: Substitute tamari for the fish sauce.] Stir to mix and serve immediately.

6. Garnish with sprigs of mint and cilantro.

Time Estimate
Hands-on, 30 minutes; unsupervised, 1 hour.

Nutritional Profile per Serving
157 calories; 4 g fat; 1 g saturated fat; 23% of calories from fat; 28 g carbohydrate; 2 g dietary fiber.

Vegetarian Option
Replace the fish sauce with low-sodium tamari.

Portability
Prepare all the ingredients and proceed through Step 3. Resealable bags make this an easy dish to transport. You might want to take a large skillet. Do the actual stir-fry just before serving so it doesn't lose its freshness.

This handy blend can be made in just a few minutes and stored in a sealed jar for use in a variety of dishes. This recipe makes about 1/2 cup.

 5 teaspoons turmeric
 1 1/2 teaspoons dry mustard
 5 teaspoons ground cumin
 5 teaspoons ground coriander
 1 1/4 teaspoons cayenne pepper
 2 1/2 teaspoons dill seeds
 2 1/2 teaspoons decorticated
  cardamom seeds
 2 1/2 teaspoons funugreek seeds

Grind to a fine powder in a small electric coffee grinder designated for this use. Shake through a sieve to remove coarse pieces or debris.

•Coconut Extract

I prefer coconut extracts or essences made from natural sources, because artificial coconut flavorings have a strong chemical smell that gives an "off" taste to an entire dish. John Wagner and Sons makes an excellent natural coconut essence that can be found in any well-stocked grocery or gourmet food store. For information, call [800] 832-9017.

Roasted Chicken with Pineapple Curry Sauce

This is quite possibly the most delicious chicken you will ever cook. The pineapple-flavored curry sauce can be used over seafood or pork or as a simple sauce for vegetables. Serve with Vegetable Stir-Fry with Passion Fruit Vinaigrette [page 131].

SERVES 6

 2 stalks fresh lemongrass, about 9 inches [23 cm] each
 1 piece gingerroot [about 4 inches or 10 cm], finely sliced
 6 cloves garlic, peeled, bashed, and chopped
 2 whole chickens, about 3 1/2 pounds [1 1/2 kg] each, rinsed and dried

Pineapple Curry Sauce
 1 teaspoon light olive oil
 3/4 cup finely diced sweet onion
 1 tablespoon India Ethmix° or good Madras curry
 1 tablespoon peeled and grated gingerroot
 2 large cloves garlic, peeled, bashed, and finely chopped
 1 tablespoon finely sliced lemongrass
 3/4 cup low-sodium chicken or vegetable stock
 1/3 cup frozen pineapple juice concentrate
 1/4 cup yogurt cheese [page 37]
 1/2 teaspoon coconut extract°
 1 tablespoon Thai fish sauce [see page 126]

Vegetarian Option [per Serving]
 1 slightly underripe banana
 1/2 teaspoon light olive oil
 1 tablespoon low-sodium tamari

To Prepare the Chickens
 1. Preheat the oven to 350 degrees F [180 degrees C].

 2. Remove the tough outside layer of the lemongrass stalk and cut off the root end and the dry top. Starting from the root end, cut the most tender, bulb-like part of the stalk into thin diagonal slices.

3. Combine the lemongrass, ginger, and garlic and divide between the cavities of the two chickens. Turn the chickens breast down on a plate so that the seasonings fall against the inside of the breasts. Insert a vertical poultry roaster* into each chicken and stand upright. Tie the legs together with cotton string and tuck the wings behind the breast. Set the chickens in a 9x13-inch [23x33-cm] baking dish.

4. If you don't have a vertical roaster, lay the chickens on a rack in a roasting pan. Tie the legs together with cotton string and tuck the wings behind the breast.

5. Whichever roasting method you are using, pour 1½ cups of warm water into the bottom of the baking dish. Bake in the preheated oven for 45 minutes to 1 hour, or until the chickens reach 140 degrees F [60 degrees C] in the thickest part of the thigh.* [The chickens in the roasting pan may take an extra 10 minutes.] Remove from the oven and set aside for 10 minutes. The final internal temperatue should be 160 degrees F [70 degrees C].

To Prepare the Sauce

6. Warm the oil in a medium saucepan over medium heat. Sauté the onion and India Ethmix until the onion is soft and translucent, about 5 minutes. Stir in the ginger, garlic, and lemongrass and cook for 3 more minutes.

7. Add the chicken stock and pineapple juice concentrate, stirring to incorporate. [Vegetarian Option: Use vegetable stock.] Cook for an additional 3 minutes. Strain the sauce through a sieve into a small saucepan using a purée press or the back of a spoon.

8. Whisk together the yogurt cheese, coconut extract, and Thai fish sauce in a 2-cup glass measure. Pour a little of the hot pineapple sauce into the yogurt mixture and stir to warm the yogurt cheese. Add the tempered yogurt cheese to the sauce and whisk until smooth. Cover and set aside to keep warm. [Vegetarian Option: Use tamari instead of fish sauce and set

*Vertical Roaster

This sensible gadget allows a chicken to roast upright in the oven. Hot oven air can circulate evenly around the bird, and the fat drains into a baking pan placed underneath [a cup of water will prevent spattering]. I prefer a clay roaster and often stuff the cavity of the chicken with fresh herbs. The pylon holds the herbs against the interior surface of the bird and imparts a great deal of flavor. Chickens roasted on a pylon cook more evenly, particularly in a convection oven, and produce juicy and flavorful results.

*Meat Thermometer

If you don't have a bayonet-type meat thermometer, it's time to get one. These thermometers read temperatures instantly, and I have found them to be quite accurate as well as inexpensive. Even the cheap ones can be reset by plunging the thermometer into boiling water [212 degrees F or 100 degrees C] and adjusting a knob at the base of the thermometer head. For an upscale choice, look for a digital thermometer; these are more expensive but easier to read. A recent issue of *Cook's Illustrated* magazine recommended the Taylor digital thermometer.

aside $^1/_4$ cup of the curry sauce per vegetarian serving before
proceeding.]

To Assemble the Dish

9. Remove the chickens from the roasting pan and pour the
   cooking juices into a fat strainer.* Remove the vertical
   roasters if you were using them. Remove and discard the skin.
   Cut the legs and breast meat away from the carcasses. Put aside
   1 leg and 1 breast for another meal. Slice the meat from the
   remaining breasts and legs and arrange on a warmed plate.
   Cover and keep warm.

10. Pour the de-fatted pan juices into a small saucepan and boil
    vigorously until the liquid is reduced to about $^1/_4$ cup. Allow to
    cool for a minute, then stir into the curry sauce.

11. Arrange slices of chicken on a warmed plate and spoon curry
    sauce over the meat. Serve Vegetable Stir-Fry with Passion
    Fruit Vinaigrette alongside.

Time Estimate
Hands-on, 30 minutes; unsupervised, approximately 1 hour.

Nutritional Profile per Serving
297 calories; 8 g fat; 2 saturated fat; 26% of calories from fat;
12 g carbohydrate; 1 g dietary fiber.

Vegetarian Option: Sautéed Bananas with Pineapple Curry Sauce
Cut a slightly underripe banana in half lengthwise and sauté for
1 or 2 minutes per side in the oil. Add a little vegetable stock to the
$^1/_4$ cup of sauce and pour over the banana.

Vegetarian Option Nutritional Profile per Serving
256 calories; 4 g fat; 0 g saturated fat; 14% of calories from fat;
52 g carbohydrate; 7 g dietary fiber.

Vegetable Stir-Fry with Passion Fruit Vinaigrette

Okay, so there are seventeen ingredients. Now, either you can see this as too many or as an extraordinary opportunity to orchestrate a rich medley of great flavors. Guess which way I saw it? Passion fruit steps forward and plays a starring role here, quite passionately. You should be able to find it, or request it, seasonally in your market.

SERVES 6

Vinaigrette

    4   fresh passion fruit*
    1/2 small shallot, finely chopped [1 teaspoon]
    1   small clove garlic, peeled, bashed, and chopped
    1/2 teaspoon honey
    1   teaspoon fresh lemon juice
    1/2 teaspoon Worcestershire sauce
    3   tablespoons rice vinegar
    1/2 teaspoon arrowroot

Vegetables

    1   teaspoon light olive oil
    6   green onions, white parts sliced [1/4 cup], green parts cut
        on the diagonal [3/4 cup]
    4   medium carrots, peeled and cut on the diagonal into
        1/4-inch [3/4-cm] slices [1 cup]
    1   medium red bell pepper, seeded and cut into 2-inch
        [5-cm] strips [1 cup]
    1   medium yellow bell pepper, seeded and cut into 2-inch
        [5-cm] strips [1 cup]
    3   cups broccoli flowerettes, cut small
    1   cup mung bean sprouts

Garnish

    6   large butter lettuce leaves

To Prepare the Vinaigrette

1. Cut each passion fruit in half and scoop the pulp and seeds into
   a small bowl.

*Passion Fruit

These small, round, dark purple fruits are native to Brazil and can be found seasonally in markets throughout the world. A ripe one should have deeply wrinkled, yellowish-orange skin with a very soft interior. Choose the largest, heaviest fruit. The seeds are edible, but if you prefer to remove them, press the pulp through a sieve or twist through a cheesecloth.

2. Put the shallot, garlic, honey, lemon juice, and Worcestershire sauce in a blender and process at high speed until smooth. Add the vinegar a little at a time as you need more liquid.

3. When all the vinegar has been added, pour the mixture into the bowl with the passion fruit pulp. Stir and press with a rubber spatula to rinse the seeds and separate them from the pulp. Pour through a medium sieve into another bowl, pressing gently but firmly with the rubber spatula to release as much pulp as you can. Stir in the arrowroot and set aside.

To Prepare the Stir-Fry

4. Warm a high-sided frying pan over medium-high heat and add the oil. Sauté the white parts of the onions for 1 minute to release their flavor. Remove the onions from the pan and set aside to save them from burning. Sauté the carrots and red and yellow peppers for 1 minute. Stir in the broccoli and reduce the heat to low. Cover the pan and cook for 1½ to 2 minutes.

5. Add the sprouts and both the white and green parts of the onions and cook until just heated through. Pour the sauce over the hot vegetables and stir until it bubbles, thickens, and develops a glossy sheen.

6. To serve, divide the stir-fry into six portions and place each serving on top of a large lettuce leaf.

Time Estimate
Hands-on, 35 minutes.

Nutritional Profile per Serving
74 calories; 1 g fat; 0 g saturated fat; 13% of calories from fat; 15 g carbohydrate; 5 g dietary fiber.

Lychee Sorbet with Fruit Salsa

It is hard to imagine a more refreshing dessert to follow the mild heat of the curry sauce. I call for canned lychees here because they are very good and are easier to find in mainland supermarkets than fresh lychees. They will still be a unique treat for many guests. This is especially wonderful served with a crisp ginger cookie made from the Fruit Basket recipe [page 179].

SERVES 6

Sorbet

- 2 cups water
- 1 tablespoon grated fresh gingerroot
- 1/2 cup sugar
- 2 cans lychees* [20 ounces or 565 g each], drained, 1/2 cup of the syrup reserved

Fruit Salsa

- 1 mango, peeled, seeded, and finely chopped [about 3/4 cup]
- 3/4 cup peeled, cored, and finely diced fresh pineapple
- 6 mint leaves, finely chopped
- 3/4 teaspoon coarsely ground black peppercorns
- 1 1/2 cups chopped, unsweetened strawberries [fresh or frozen]

To Prepare the Sorbet

1. Combine the water, ginger, and sugar in a medium saucepan and bring to a boil over high heat. Remove from the heat and strain through a fine sieve with a purée press,* discarding the ginger pulp.

2. Process the lychees and 1/2 cup of their syrup in a blender or food processor until smooth, about 2 minutes. Pour through a sieve set over the ginger water, again pressing with a purée press. Discard the pulp.

3. Freeze the lychee sauce in an ice cream freezer according to the manufacturer's directions. If you do not have an ice cream

*Lychees

This fruit is native to China and is now grown in tropical climates of the United States. It is available fresh in Asian markets during the summer months and canned year-round. The fruit is covered with a thin, brittle, slightly bumpy shell that is easily removed with your fingers. The fruit inside is white, soft, and somewhat like a grape. It has a marvelous aroma which is not lost during the canning process.

*Purée Press

I designed this tool to press food through a sieve and extract the last bit of flavor. This wooden, mushroom-shaped tool looks like my mother's darning egg, and I like to call it a "sock 'n sieve." It greatly speeds up the task of sieving food.

machine, freeze the liquid in a shallow baking pan until it is almost solid. This will take an hour or two depending on your freezer.

4. Once the sauce is frozen, remove it from the freezer and break into small pieces. Beat in the large bowl of an electric mixer until smooth. Return the mixture to the shallow pan and refreeze. Repeat the freezing and beating process until you are satisfied with the consistency of the sorbet. The more times you beat, the smoother the texture will be, but it must be refrozen each time. One short beating will produce a granità. Several beatings will result in a richer, smoother texture.

5. When you are satisfied with the texture, transfer the sorbet to a covered storage container and let it ripen in the freezer for at least 30 minutes before serving.

To Prepare the Salsa

This salsa should be made as close to serving time as possible in order to be at its best.

6. Toss the prepared mango, pineapple, mint, pepper, and strawberries in a small bowl and set aside until ready to serve. If you are using frozen strawberries, chop and add them at the last minute, still partially frozen, so they don't become limp.

To Serve

7. Place a scoop of the sorbet on a chilled dessert plate. Spoon $1/3$ cup of the fruit salsa alongside and garnish with a crisp ginger cookie.

Time Estimate

Hands-on, 30 minutes; unsupervised, 20 to 30 minutes depending on your ice cream machine; 2-3 hours using a freezer.

Nutritional Profile per Serving [*not including cookies*]

231 calories; 0 g fat; 0 g saturated fat; 1% of calories from fat; 59 g carbohydrate; 1 g dietary fiber.

Portability

Prepare the sorbet ahead and leave it in the insulated insert of your ice cream machine or pack it into a plastic storage container. If it is frozen very hard, remove it from the freezer 30 minutes to an hour before serving so it will be "scoopable." You can make the salsa at home, but do it just before you leave so it will stay fresh, and if you're using frozen strawberries, remember not to add them until the last minute. The cookies can be made up to a week ahead and stored in an airtight plastic container.

salad
Pohole or Sunflower Sprout Salad
Beautiful blend of fiddlehead ferns with a delicate tamari dressing.

main course
Tofu and Mushrooms in a Spicy Miso Sauce
Creative combination of dark miso and ginger, anise and red peppers, create a rich and satisfying dish.

Taro and Chile Cakes
Smooth taro blended with onions and chiles, then baked to a golden brown.

vegetable
Steamed Baby Bok Choy
Delectable little cabbage greens steamed to bring out their perfect freshness.

Kabocha Squash
Wonderful Japanese pumpkin with a golden nutty flesh gets a brush of tamari and a sprinkle of pepper.

dessert
Pineapple Dessert Crêpes
Delicate, creamy, and fruit-filled with a touch of Kona coffee dusted on the pineapple scented sauce.

travelogue

*A*n interesting thing about our arrival in Honolulu was that the Queen Elizabeth II docked downtown. I mean that literally. We pulled into a slip just a few steps from a traffic intersection, and I expected the harbormaster to call out, "Watch for the Aloha Tower on Pier 9, hang a left, and stop at the first intersection."

Honolulu is an old whaling port on the island of Oahu, which is a Hawaiian word meaning "the gathering place," a fact that we discovered after we had named this book. Oahu is the most populated of the islands, referred to by many as a melting pot of Hawaiian, Asian, Portuguese, and Filipino cultures. I prefer to think of the cultures here as "melding" more than melting. There

OAHU
The Gathering Place

is no loss of cultural identity, but a joining of traditions in the true acceptance and warmth of "Aloha."

This is not to say that cultural differences do not exist and that native Hawaiians do not regret the passing of a certain part of their cultural identity. However, from the streets of modern Honolulu, one might conclude that the dominant culture is that of the tourist,

Honolulu is an old whaling port on the island of Oahu, which is a Hawaiian word meaning "the gathering place"

which helps to explain why Honolulu has such a bewildering array of places to eat. The food is delicious, or as locals would say, "onolicious." Island favorites include black sugar donuts at Ting Yin Bakery, fruit shakes at Ruffage, malasadas [hole-free Portuguese donuts] at Leonard's Bakery, manapua [steamed whole wheat buns with meatless fillings] at Broke the Mouth, or poi at Ala Moana Farmers' Market.

In case you have never tasted poi, it is simply a paste made from mashed cooked taro roots—the same tubers that the first Polynesian settlers ate on their long ocean voyage in their open canoes and that they planted in their new home. Captain Cook visited tidy fields of taro and other crops on his first visit to Hawaii, and the islanders treated his crew to roasted meat and samples of poi. [Not all of the sailors asked for second helpings.] The natives called the taro plant Haloa, which means everlasting breath, and both its leaves and roots are traditional staples of the Hawaiian diet. The heart-shaped leaves, or *lu'au*, were cooked as greens, and the roots were baked, boiled, or steamed in underground ovens. The plant was also used for medicinal purposes. The stems, called *haha*, were rubbed on insect bites, while the leaves were made into poultices to treat injuries. Poi was prescribed for upset stomachs and was also applied to infected sores. Taro was vital to the survival of the Hawaiian people, and they considered it a sacred plant. There was an annual feast to celebrate the first ripe taro root harvested each year, and many important rituals were centered around the poi bowl. Under the strict divisions of labor that governed their society, only men were allowed to plant and harvest the taro and prepare the poi. In modern Hawaii, women are allowed to touch the plant, yet poi remains an important element of the culture. It is often the first solid food given to babies and is still regarded as "soul food" by many islanders.

After finishing our own research on poi, Treena and I set out to learn more about other island foods, particularly ones that could be adapted for people who want to eat on the "lighter side." We were fortunate to meet up with Paul Onishi, a Honolulu restaurateur who graciously spent the entire day showing us the flip side of indulgence. We followed him to Chinese markets, where he explained the ancient arts of healing and preventive health care. We visited a small, family-owned miso factory and I came away an enthusiastic proponent of this traditional Japanese flavor base, useful in so many dishes.

Our day ended after a short drive inland to Paul's restaurant, the Waioli Tea Room, set amongst one of the most beautiful tropical gardens I have ever seen. In the nostalgic days before airplanes and massive cruise ships, this tea room was *the* place to come. Tea was the social beverage of choice, and the Salvation Army ran the place with extreme gentility. Today, the tea room is still a quiet, serene gathering place for those who love to celebrate the flavors of east and west.

During our visit to Honolulu, we also became acquainted with Dr. Terry Shintani, a notable physician and author of the original *Eat More, Weigh Less* [you may recall the title was inadvertently used later by Dr. Dean Ornish]. Dr. Shintani is associated with the Waianae Coast Comprehensive Health Center, where his master's degree in nutrition is being put to good use. He has done innovative

Previous page:
Popular deli "Broke the Mouth" and its specialty: filled whole wheat rolls.

Facing page, from top:
We tour Honolulu markets.

Our friend Paul Onishi, a Honolulu resaurateur, is a knowledgeable guide.

The Waioli Tea Room and Restaurant offers a restful island retreat.

This page, from top:
We visit a traditional miso factory.

Terry Shintani, M.D. [*below, left*] is a wealth of nutritional information and innovative ideas.

This dinner draws upon the foods of the many cultures that have melded in modern Hawaii.

research showing that a diet based on traditional Hawaiian foods—before the days of Spam and fast food—can reduce weight and body fat, lower cholesterol and blood pressure, and result in a better insulin balance. Dr. Shintani continues to work on creative seasonings and techniques that will make basic island foods more appealing to a wider audience.

We learned a great deal from Dr. Shintani and from Paul Onishi and his talented staff, as well as from the time we spent resting in the coolness of the island tea room. We have tried to apply that insight to a dinner that draws upon the foods of the many cultures that have melded in modern Hawaii. It begins with a simple salad of native *pohole* [fiddlehead ferns], dressed with a splash of tamari

and rice vinegar. The main dish is tofu, braised in miso and mushroom sauce and served alongside a spicy, soft Taro and Chile Cake, steamed baby bok choy and the nutty, golden kabocha squash. For dessert, delicate crêpes are topped with a sauté of fresh pineapple and a creamy sauce fragrant with a hint of Kona coffee. If you and your friends have begun to experiment with vegetarian menus, this would make a very good choice for a dinner party. The entire meal has 643 calories with 9 grams of fat, a very healthy 13% of calories from fat, only 1 gram of which is saturated.

Pohole or Sunflower Sprout Salad

Pohole [pronounced po-HOH-lay] is a fiddlehead fern that grows prolifically in Hawaii's rain forests. The young fronds are beautiful, delicate, and hold up quite nicely in a salad. You'll need to special order, which may take two weeks or so. However, sunflower sprouts make a fine substitute for this crisp and colorful salad.

SERVES 6

Salad

1 pound [450 g] *pohole** or 9 ounces [255 grams] sunflower sprouts

1 bunch green onions

1/2 cup fresh pomegranate seeds* or dried cranberries

Dressing

1 tablespoon tamari*

2 tablespoons rice vinegar*

1/8 teaspoon Shanghai Ethmix* [*see page* 142]

1. Remove the heavy stalks from the bottom of the *pohole* and discard. Break the remaining fronds into 1-inch [2½-cm] pieces. If you are using sunflower sprouts, wash and cut off any brown parts.

2. Cut off the white parts of the onions and set aside for another use. Wash the green parts, then slice into 1-inch [2½-cm] pieces. Combine the *pohole* or sprouts with the sliced onion greens in a salad bowl.

3. Combine the tamari, rice vinegar, and Shanghai Ethmix, and toss with the greens. Sprinkle the pomegranate seeds or dried cranberries over the top.

4. Serve on chilled salad plates.

Time Estimate

Hands-on, 20 minutes.

*Pohole

This is a special treat for your guests that is worth pursuing. It is available year round from:

René and Eileen Comeaux
Hana Herbs
P.O. Box 323
Hana, Maui, Hawaii 96713
Phone or fax: [808] 248-7407

*Pomegranate

This fruit turns up in our supermarkets in fall and early winter and keeps well if refrigerated. The tart seeds provide a wonderful brightness and interesting texture to many dishes. Paula Wolfort, a notable expert on Middle Eastern and Mediterranean cuisines, suggests separating the seeds from the pulp in a bowl of water; the seeds sink and the pulp floats.

*Tamari

This high-quality Japanese soy sauce derives its rich flavor from amino acids and soy protein. It is made from fermenting soybeans with little or no wheat and is stronger in flavor and darker in color than other Japanese soy sauces. It contains no alcohol, so it can be simmered without its flavor evaporating. Kikkoman makes a low-sodium version which you may find in your supermarket, an Asian market, or a natural food store.

*Rice Vinegar

You'll have no trouble finding this in your local supermarket. Made in China and Japan, it is more mellow than distilled vinegar. Cider vinegar is an acceptable substitute.

• Shanghai Ethmix

    7 tablespoons crushed red
       pepper flakes
    2$\frac{1}{2}$ teaspoons ground ginger
    2$\frac{1}{2}$ teaspoons ground anise

Grind to a fine powder in a small electric coffee grinder designated for this purpose. Store excess in a sealed jar.

Nutritional Profile per Serving

47 calories; 0 g fat; 0 g saturated fat; 5% of calories from fat; 8 g carbohydrate; 0 g dietary fiber.

Portability

Prepare the *pohole* or sunflower sprouts at home and combine with the onions. Refrigerate in a large resealable bag. The dressing can be made in advance and brought to the party in a sealed jar. Remove the pomegranate seeds from the pulp and carry in a small resealable bag. The dried cranberries are easy to carry the same way.

Tofu and Mushrooms in a Spicy Miso Sauce

An "onolicious" combination of soft textures balanced by the richness of dark miso and the brightness of ginger, star anise, and hot chile peppers. If you are looking for a creative way to experiment with tofu, this could be it. Serve with Taro and Chile Cakes [page 145], Steamed Baby Bok Choy [page 147], and Kabocha Squash [page 148].

SERVES 6

1½	teaspoons light olive oil
1	large clove garlic, peeled, bashed, and chopped
½	onion, thinly sliced
1½	cups plus 2 tablespoons dashi broth*
¼	teaspoon dried basil
2	teaspoons hatcho miso,* mixed with 1 tablespoon water
¼	teaspoon Shanghai Ethmix* [page 142]
10½	ounces [294 g] extra-firm light tofu,* cut into 1-inch [2½-cm] cubes [see page 144]
¼	pound [112 g] fresh shiitake mushrooms, stemmed and halved
½	pound [225 g] large white mushrooms, cut into 3 thick slices top to bottom
¼	teaspoon salt
¼	teaspoon freshly ground black pepper
1	tablespoon fresh lemon juice
1	tablespoon chopped fresh parsley
4	teaspoons arrowroot

1. Warm ½ teaspoon of the oil in a medium saucepan over medium-high heat. Sauté the garlic and onion for 5 minutes, or until the onion is soft but not browned. Stir in 1½ cups of the dashi broth and the basil. Simmer for 3 minutes.

2. Strain the mixture and return the liquid to the saucepan, discarding the onion. Add the thinned miso, Shanghai Ethmix, and tofu. Set aside.

3. Warm the remaining teaspoon of oil in a large frying pan over medium-high heat. Add the shiitake and white mushrooms,

*Dashi Broth

This simple stock is easy to make and handy for soups, stews, or dips for tempura. Ingredients may be found at an Asian market or a well-stocked supermarket.

  6 inch piece kombu
  3 dried shiitake mushrooms
  7 cups water

Soak the kombu and mushrooms in water for 15 minutes. Remove the mushrooms, cut off and discard the stems and thinly slice the caps. Return mushroom caps to water; remove kombu just before water boils. Simmer gently for five minutes. Remove the mushroom caps and reserve them and the kombu for another use.

*Hatcho Miso

Miso is a fermented soybean product that is essential to Japanese cooking. Low in calories and a good source of amino acids, vitamins, and minerals, miso enhances the flavor of soups, sauces, and other dishes. Hatcho miso is a special miso that has been made by the Hatcho Miso Company in Okazaki, Japan, for five centuries. It is made in the traditional way with whole soybeans and a small amount of water and has 80% more protein and 25% less salt than rice and barley misos. You will find it sold under labels such as Mitoku Macrobiotic, Erewhon, Westbrae, and Tree of Life at your supermarket or a good natural foods store.

After experimenting with this versatile product, I have found that I prefer Mori-Nu Lite Silken Tofu. It is low in fat and calories and doesn't need to be refrigerated. You will find it in natural food stores or good supermarkets. I like the extra-firm variety in most recipes.

sprinkle with the salt and pepper, and cook for 2 minutes. Sprinkle the lemon juice over the top and cook for an additional 2 minutes. Stir in the parsley, then add the tofu and dashi broth mixture.

4. Combine the arrowroot with the remaining 2 tablespoons of dashi broth to make a slurry. Remove the frying pan from the heat and add the slurry, then return to the heat and stir until thickened and glossy.

5. Serve on a warmed plate with two taro and chile cakes, a portion of bok choy, and a wedge of kabocha squash.

Time Estimate
Hands-on, 30 minutes.

Nutritional Profile per Serving
67 calories; 2 g fat; 0 g saturated fat; 28% of calories from fat; 8 g carbohydrate; 1 g dietary fiber.

Taro and Chile Cakes

These neat, tasty patties are very much like crab cakes. We enjoyed a similar version in Honolulu and they are typical of the creative work being done by contemporary chefs who use traditional foods in new ways. You should be able to find taro root in a supermarket with a good produce department, or you can substitute red potatoes, although your results will be a more conventional potato pancake.

SERVES 6

1³/₄	pounds [800 g] taro root* or red potatoes
1	teaspoon light olive oil
1	large sweet onion, finely diced
2	jalapeño peppers, cored, seeded, and finely diced
¹/₂	cup egg substitute
¹/₂	teaspoon salt
1	large carrot, grated
3	tablespoons chopped fresh parsley
¹/₂	cup all-purpose flour

1. Place the taro roots in a large steamer, cover, and steam for 30 to 40 minutes, or until very tender. Cover with cold water, then peel when cool enough to handle. Cut each taro root into several pieces and beat with an electric mixer until it has the consistency of smooth paste.

2. Preheat the oven to 450 degrees F [230 degrees C].

3. Warm the oil in a large frying pan over medium heat. Sauté the onion and jalapeños until very soft but not browned, about 10 minutes.

4. Add the egg substitute, salt, carrot, and parsley to the taro paste. Add the onion mixture and combine well.

5. Cover a large plate with the flour. Scoop about twelve ¹/₈-cup balls of the taro mixture onto the plate and dust with flour. Using the palm of your hand, flatten each ball into a patty about ¹/₂ inch [1¹/₂ cm] thick. Lay the patties on a greased cookie sheet.

*Taro Root

This tuber probably originated in East India, although it is used in the Pacific Islands, Asia, the Caribbean, North Africa, and parts of Central and South America. Its texture is somewhere between potatoes and chestnuts. After peeling, it can be steamed and lightly mashed or stir-fried. I order taro root from my local produce manager, but you may also find it in Asian markets. You may want to wear gloves when you peel the roots as they may irritate your skin.

6. Lightly coat the tops of the cakes with cooking spray and bake in the preheated oven for 10 minutes. Turn the patties and bake for 10 minutes more, or until golden brown.

7. Serve two cakes per person.

Time Estimate
Hands-on, 30 minutes; unsupervised, 1 hour.

Nutritional Profile per Serving
232 calories; 1 g fat; 0 g saturated fat; 4% of calories from fat; 51 g carbohydrate; 7 g dietary fiber.

Steamed Baby Bok Choy

These most delectable members of the Chinese cabbage family are especially tasty when they are young and tender. No added flavors are needed here, just the sweetness, color, and freshness of perfectly steamed greens.

SERVES 6

> 6 heads baby bok choy,* cut in half lengthwise
> 1/4 teaspoon salt
> 1/4 teaspoon pepper

Lay the bok choy halves in a large steamer and sprinkle with the salt and pepper. Cover and steam for 3 minutes, or until tender-crisp.

Time Estimate
Hands-on, 10 minutes.

Nutritional Profile per Serving
9 calories; 0 g fat; 0 g saturated fat; 11% of calories from fat; 1 g carbohydrate; 0 g dietary fiber.

*Bok Choy

I love this Asian member of the cabbage family. Its thick white stem is crunchy and its leaves are the tiniest bit bitter—a great combination in a single vegetable. This recipe calls for baby bok choy, but you'll want to try the larger leaves and stems in other recipes.

Kabocha Squash

This small, round Japanese pumpkin has dark green skin with grayish stripes. Its golden nutty taste is truly wonderful, as is the abundance of vitamins A and C and potassium in its bright orange flesh. Kabocha squash may be available in your local market in fall and winter, or you may substitute another golden-fleshed squash such as butternut or acorn.

SERVES 6

1   kabocha or butternut squash, about 3 pounds [1350 g]
1   tablespoon low-sodium tamari* [*see page 141*]
1/4   teaspoon white pepper

1. Preheat the oven to 350 degrees F [180 degrees C].

2. Remove the stem and cut the squash in half from top to bottom. Discard the seeds and stringy center and cut each half into 3 wedges. Brush each wedge with tamari, sprinkle with pepper, and coat lightly with cooking spray.

3. Bake for 40 minutes in the preheated oven.

Time Estimate
Hands-on, 10 minutes; unsupervised, 40 minutes.

Nutritional Profile per Serving
77 calories; 1 g fat; 0 g saturated fat; 12% of calories from fat; 17 g carbohydrate; 0 g dietary fiber.

Pineapple Crêpes

It is hard to play favorites with desserts, but I have to say I am very partial to this one. It is delicate and creamy, yet freshly fruited— exactly what we are looking for in a light and scrumptious dessert. The touch of Kona coffee in the wine-scented pineapple sauce is just plain "kupaianaha" [that's Hawaiian for wonderful]. There are a number of low-fat ways that crêpes can be used in desserts and main courses and I urge you to explore them. If you're not an expert, you might want to practice with your crêpe technique—you should be able to read the New York Times through them.

SERVES 6

Crêpe Batter
- 1 whole egg
- 1 egg yolk
- 1 cup 2% milk
- 1/2 teaspoon vanilla extract
- 1/2 cup all-purpose flour
- 1 teaspoon light olive oil

Pineapple Sauce
- 1/2 teaspoon light oil
- 1 lime, zest cut into thin strips
- 1/3 cup pineapple juice concentrate
- 2/3 cup water
- 3/4 cup plus 2 tablespoons fruity white wine [I prefer dealcoholized white zinfandel]
- 2 tablespoons chopped crystallized ginger
- 1 tablespoon brown sugar
- 1 tablespoon cornstarch
- 1/2 cup yogurt cheese* [*page 37*]
- 3 slices of fresh pineapple, 1/4 inch [3/4 cm] thick, cut into quarters [reserve the best-looking leaves]

Garnish
  Instant coffee granules or a few ground coffee beans
  Reserved pineapple leaves

To Prepare the Crêpes

1. Beat the whole egg, egg yolk, milk, and vanilla in a large bowl. Whisk in the flour, then let the batter rest for 30 minutes before cooking.

2. When you are ready to cook the crêpes, warm a crêpe pan or an 8-inch [20-cm] nonstick frying pan with low sides over medium heat. Add the oil and swirl it around to coat the bottom of the pan, then pour the excess into the batter. It is important that the skillet be good and warm before cooking the crêpes.

3. Pour ¼ cup of batter into the skillet and gently tilt the pan back and forth to coat the bottom. When the top dulls and turns waxy, 30 to 45 seconds, turn the crêpe over and cook the other side for about 15 seconds. When done, slip the crêpe onto a paper towel, light side up.

4. Repeat this process with the remaining batter, spraying the pan with cooking spray if needed to keep the crêpes from sticking. When all the crêpes are cooked, wrap them in a cloth napkin, where they will keep quite well for at least six hours.

To Prepare the Sauce

5. Warm the oil in a 10-inch [25-cm] nonstick skillet over medium-high heat. Sauté the lime zest for about 1 minute to extract the volatile oils. Add the pineapple juice concentrate, water, and ½ cup of the wine. Simmer for 6 minutes.

6. Strain the sauce into a small saucepan, discarding the zest. Add the crystallized ginger and brown sugar and stir over medium heat until the sugar dissolves.

7. Combine the cornstarch with 2 tablespoons of the wine to make a slurry. Pull the pan off the heat and stir in the slurry, then return to the heat and stir until thickened and clear.

8. Spoon the yogurt cheese into a 2-cup glass measure and add a small amount of the warm sauce to temper the yogurt. Whisk until completely smooth, then add the rest of the sauce.

9. Rinse the saucepan with the remaining ¼ cup of wine and pour the liquid into the skillet. Stir in the yogurt sauce over very low

heat. Place one cooked crêpe in the sauce and coat well on both sides. Using a spoon and a fork, fold the crêpe into quarters [the crêpe will be in the shape of a triangle]. Move the folded crêpe to the side of the pan. Repeat the coating and folding process with the remaining crêpes.

To Serve

10. Place two crêpes per serving on warmed dessert plates. Add the pineapple slices to the sauce remaining in the pan and warm them through, then spoon two pieces of pineapple alongside the crêpes. Dust with coffee granules and garnish with pineapple leaves.

Time Estimate

Hands-on, 45 minutes; unsupervised, 30 minutes.

Nutritional Profile per Serving

211 calories; 4 g fat; 1 g saturated fat; 16% of calories from fat; 37 g carbohydrate; 1 g dietary fiber.

Portability

This recipe can be made ahead through Step 7. Bring the thickened sauce in the pan you cooked it in and don't forget the frying pan you will use to finish the dessert. Carry the liquids in containers with tight-fitting lids. You might want to bring along your whisk and 2-cup glass measure. Carry the pineapple slices and garnish in separate resealable bags.

salad
Island Greens Salad with Papaya Seed Dressing
Napa cabbage with crispy vegetables and smooth, ripe papaya.

main course
Palusamis
Collard greens wrap around fresh tuna for an engaging taste and dramatic presentation.

vegetarian option
Plantain and Pineapple Wrapped with Greens

vegetable
Green Bean Rice Pilau
Rice cooked in flavorful stock and perked up with the tastes of cardamom, turmeric, and other Indian spices.

dessert
Koko Tapioca with Bananas and Crystallized Ginger
Sinful chocolate custard healthfully lightened with tapioca, ginger, and bananas.

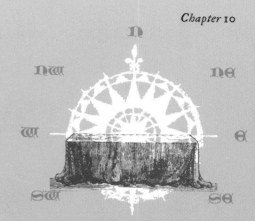

travelogue

As our ship pulled away from its Honolulu berth, we looked forward to the coming voyage, not knowing we would be toyed with by a rather playful Neptune. We spent four days on choppy seas as we made our way over twenty-five hundred miles southwest.

The small chain of volcanic islands known as the Samoas lies in the heart of the South Pacific and is considered by their inhabitants to be the cradle of Polynesian culture. Indeed, archaeologists have found village sites dating back to 1,000 B.C., and anthropologists speculate that these original seafarers migrated from Southeast Asia. The first written records of the islands come from a French explorer of 1768. Impressed by the nautical ability of the islanders, who sailed their small canoes far from the sight of land, he christened their home the Navigator Islands.

AMERICAN SAMOA
High Palms and A Gentle Sea

Christian missionaries arrived in the 1800s to convert the Navigators and were well-received. A London missionary named John Williams was especially effective in bringing an end to tribal wars, which he managed to replace with dance competitions and dugout canoe races. If only he could have convinced the foreign nations who were squabbling over the Samoas to take out their frustrations in a dugout race, we would have a different story to tell. By the end of the 19th century, Germany and the United States had developed conflicting interests in the Samoas, a situation which was

I was especially impressed by the feeling of family and community called "fa'asamoa" [way of life].

finally resolved by dividing the islands along the 171st meridian into Western Samoa [under German rule] and American Samoa. In 1962 Western Samoa became the first independent island nation in the Pacific, while American Samoa continues to be administered by the United States.

One of the things you will learn within moments of stepping ashore in American Samoa is the proper way to pronounce the name of the wonderful country: "Ahhhmeeereckaaan Samoooaah." Although most Samoans speak English, they apply the double-vowel sounds of their native language to many words, giving their speech a soothing, lilting quality.

Our arrival in the capital city of Pago Pago [pronounced Pango Pango], was astonishing. Even though the city is one of the best ports in the Pacific, this was the first time the Queen Elizabeth II had visited. Clearly this was big stuff, and to mark the occasion, they had a fifty-foot banner prominently displayed: "Welcome, Graham and Treena Kerr!" We were met by a television crew who managed to produce a half-hour special on our visit and have it on the air before we departed ten hours later!

Our guide for the visit was Sinira Fuimaono, a captivating island beauty whose enthusiasm for Ahhhmeeereckaaan Samoooaaah was the best introduction anyone could have. Sinira knew everything and everybody and had engineered the display of the banner. She had planned an ambitious schedule for us, including a visit to an outdoor market, an organic farm [where we sampled delicious miniature pineapples], an interview with Peter Gurr, the Minister of Agriculture, and lunch with Governor and Mrs. A. P. Lutali. We

Previous page:
Sinira Fuimaona is a knowledgeable guide.
A squeeze of lemon into a coconut: delicious.

This page, from top:
A fifty foot banner heralds our arrival.
Sinira seems to know everything and everyone.
Breadfruit heaped for sale at the market.

even managed a side trip to meet the retired prime minister, who is doing some splendid research on organic vegetables that are suited to the Samoan climate.

Wherever we went, we were greeted with warmth and generosity. I was especially impressed by the feeling of family and community called *fa'asamoa* [way of life]. Family elders called *matai* oversee each village and ensure a sense of well-being. Most Samoan villages maintain the tradition of a short daily devotional called *sa*. You will hear a gong sound in the early evening. This is a call to prayer and a signal for all activity, including traffic, to cease. A second gong marks the beginning of prayer time. It is respectful to be quiet at this time. After ten or fifteen minutes, a third gong announces that *sa* is over.

I like this tradition very much, but it does sometimes cause an interruption in a game of *kirikiti*, which is the Samoan version of cricket, and an interesting version it is. Some people think that cricket began here in the islands and was imported to Britain, with the addition of quite a few extra regulations. As a former cricket enthusiast, I immensely enjoyed the exhibition I watched, although I never did quite figure out all the rules. Each match had a different number of players and was accompanied by rhythmic clapping and tempo whistling by the fielders, except for the moments between the time the ball was bowled [pitched] and hit.

By the time the *kirikiti* match was over, it was time for a snack, and Treena and I set off in search of another miniature pineapple and another taste of Samoan food. The traditional diet of Samoa

In honor of the lovely Samoan people and the sheer beauty of their world, I'm delighted to offer this Polynesian menu.

is quite simple and is based, naturally, on fish and other seafood, local fruits, and the ever-present taro and sweet potato. One of the Samoans' special meals handed down through generations is a wonderful dish called palusamis, in which vegetables or pieces of fish or meat are liberally sauced with coconut cream, then wrapped in taro leaves. Traditionally palusamis were baked in an earthen oven filled with hot stones and covered with layers of banana leaves. According to early visitors to the islands, the cooking was done by the men, "all chatting away merrily and freely."

This page, from top:
Governor and Mrs. A.P. Lutali give us a royal welcome at a lovely banquet.

Miss American Samoa performs.

The retired prime minister is doing splendid research on organic vegetables.

We sampled many dishes, all of which seemed to contain coconut cream, the rich layer which rises to the top of coconut milk. Anyone who has ever eaten coconut cream will understand why it is such a popular sauce, for its rich, sweet flavor enhances simple ingredients. But there is one drawback—it is very high in saturated fat. The widespread use of coconut cream, plus the addition of popular Western convenience foods, has resulted in alarming rates of diabetes, heart disease, and obesity among Samoans. So much so that a program called the "Healthy Islands Project" has been set up to address the problem. I am looking for good news from this project, which promises to help people enjoy a lighter version of many of the foods they love.

As Treena and I reboarded the ship in Pago Pago, laden with gifts of tapa cloth, kava bowls, and a cornucopia of local fruit and vegetables, we felt quite overwhelmed by the hospitality we had been shown. We read the words of poet Rupert Brooke, which now had special meaning to us:

"You lie on a mat in a cool Samoa hut and look out on the white sand under the high palms and a gentle sea, the black line of reef a mile out with moonlight over everything. And then amongst it all are the loveliest people in the world, moving and dancing like gods and goddesses. It is sheer beauty, so pure it is difficult to breathe it in."

In honor of the lovely Samoan people and the sheer beauty of their world, I'm delighted to offer this Polynesian menu, beginning with an island salad drenched in papaya-seed dressing. For an entrée, I've prepared the traditional palusamis using fresh tuna and my own version of coconut cream. My dessert invention blends tapioca with cocoa and bananas in a layered custard that looks great and tastes great, too.

The entire menu is less than 800 calories and has only 17 grams of fat. That's 19% of calories from fat [only 17% if you choose the vegetarian option].

Island Greens Salad
with Papaya Seed Dressing

American Samoa, simply put, is green: lush, deep, lavishly green with flowers and fruits and vegetables abounding. This green salad, spangled by a singular splash of color from thick slices of papaya, is a tribute to the island's abundance and color. Papaya is a wonderfully versatile fruit that I use often in salads and desserts as well as in salsas or as a "brightener" for low-fat chicken and fish dishes. Papaya was described by Christopher Columbus as "the fruit of the angels," and culinary explorers have been echoing his words ever since. These luscious "tree melons" thrive in the Samoan climate and sometimes grow as large as twenty-five pounds in the tropical sun. I suggest you look for fruit a trifle smaller than that; one about the size of a large pear will be fine.

SERVES 6

Salad

1	head napa cabbage, washed and cored
1/3	English cucumber
6	green onions, cut diagonally into 1/2-inch [1 1/2-cm] pieces
1	cup loosely packed mung bean sprouts, rinsed
4	cups washed and stemmed spinach
30	small cilantro leaves, very finely sliced
1	lime, peeled, sectioned, and chopped, juice reserved
2	tablespoons pumpkin seeds
1	large, ripe papaya, peeled and cut into 1/2-inch [1 1/2-cm] cubes or scooped into balls with a melon baller* [reserve the seeds]

Papaya Seed Dressing

4	thin slices of peeled gingerroot, about 1/4-inch [2 1/2-cm] thick
2	cloves garlic, peeled and thinly sliced
1	teaspoon mustard powder
1	tablespoon papaya seeds [optional]
1/2	cup rice vinegar [*page 141*]
1/4	cup light olive oil

*Melon Baller

This old-fashioned tool hasn't changed much over the years. I like the ones with a different size scoop on each end of a plastic or wooden handle. Melon balls are a bit "fiddly," but they finish a dish nicely. If you prefer, cubed fruit is certainly acceptable.

1 tablespoon brown sugar

1 tablespoon low-sodium tamari

To Prepare the Salad

1. Pick out six of the nicest, largest cabbage leaves and refrigerate the rest for another use. Cut out the white stems and slice them crosswise into strips. You should have about 1 cup. Wrap the leaves loosely in a towel and refrigerate.

2. Peel the cucumber and trim the sides flat so that it forms a long rectangle, then cut into a ½-inch [1½-cm] dice.

3. Put the cabbage stems, cucumber, onions, sprouts, spinach, cilantro, lime, lime juice, and pumpkin seeds in a large salad spinner. Add the papaya and toss gently. Refrigerate the ingredients in the salad spinner until ready to serve.

To Prepare the Dressing

4. Process the ginger, garlic, mustard, papaya seeds, rice vinegar, oil, brown sugar, and tamari in a blender at high speed for about 1 minute.

To Serve

5. Pour the dressing over the greens in the salad spinner. Give the spinner a few good turns to allow the extra dressing to spin off. Collect the dressing from the bottom of the spinner and sprinkle 2 tablespoons over the top of the greens. The leftover dressing will keep in the refrigerator for several days. [I often use this technique for dressing green salads. The spinner distributes the dressing evenly over the greens, and the excess doesn't collect on the leaves near the bottom, as often happens in a salad bowl.]

6. Place a chilled cabbage leaf on each salad plate and arrange a portion of the salad on top.

Time Estimate
Hands-on, 30 minutes.

Nutritional Profile per Serving

88 calories; 4 g fat; 1 g saturated fat; 45% of calories from fat; 11 g carbohydrate; 4 g dietary fiber.

Portability

Prepare the salad through Step 3 and carry to the party in the salad spinner or a large resealable bag. Make the dressing ahead and transport in a container with a tight lid. The cabbage leaves can go in another large resealable bag filled with air.

Palusamis

Without question this is the best known dish of the Samoan Islands. The classic is made of tinned corned beef wrapped in taro leaves with a very rich coconut cream. I've substituted collard leaves for taro leaves and fresh tuna in lieu of corned beef. And I've concocted my own lighter version of coconut cream that still has plenty of pungent flavor. Serve Green Bean Pilau [page 164] as your vegetable dish.

SERVES 6

Coconut Cream

3/4	cup plus 2 tablespoons 2% milk
1/2	teaspoon sugar
2	tablespoons desiccated coconut*
1	tablespoon cornstarch
1/2	teaspoon coconut essence

Palusamis

6	taro roots or red potatoes, about 2 ounces [56 g] each
1/3	to 1/2 fresh pineapple, about 6 ounces [168 g], peeled and cored
18	large collard leaves [2 bunches]
1 1/2	teaspoons light olive oil
6	ounces [168 g] Canadian bacon, cut into 1/4 x 2-inch [3/4 x 5-cm] julienne
2	green onions, white parts only, cut into 1/4-inch [3/4-cm] slices
2	tablespoons plus 1 1/2 teaspoons fresh lime juice
1/4	teaspoon dried crushed red pepper flakes
18	ounces [500 g] fresh tuna,* cut into 6 pieces

Garnish

2	fresh tomatoes, cut into 12 thin slices

Vegetarian Option [per Serving]

1/2	teaspoon light olive oil
1/2	plantain, peeled and sliced
1	ounce pineapple, cut into 1/4-inch [3/4-cm] matchsticks

•Desiccated coconut

This is simply coconut that has been dried, thus concentrating its flavor. It can be found in specialty and natural food stores.

•Tuna

Yellowfin tuna, called *Ahi* in Hawaii, often is eaten raw as sashimi or served quite rare. When cooked, it is darker than albacore and lighter than bluefin. It is usually available, fresh or frozen, in supermarket fish departments throughout the U.S. If you don't see it, ask your fishmonger to order it for you.

2 green onions, white parts only, cut into $1/4$-inch [$3/4$-cm] slices

1 taro root, about 2 ounces [55 g], peeled and boiled

$1/4$ teaspoon fresh lime juice

$1/16$ teaspoon salt

$1/16$ teaspoon chipotle sauce

3 collard leaves, trimmed and blanched

2 tablespoons coconut cream

To Prepare the Coconut Cream

1. Combine the milk, sugar, and coconut in a small saucepan and simmer over medium heat for 10 minutes. Strain the coconut and return the liquid to the pan.

2. Combine the cornstarch with the remaining 2 tablespoons of milk to make a slurry. Add the slurry to the warm milk and stir over medium heat until it thickens. Add the coconut essence and pour the mixture into a flat metal pan. Put in the refrigerator to cool.

To Prepare the Filling

3. Place the taro roots in a large steamer, cover, and steam for 30 minutes, or until tender. Rinse under cold water until cool enough to handle, then peel with a paring knife. Cut the roots into $1/4$ x 2-inch [$3/4$ x 5-cm] julienne.

4. Cut the fresh pineapple into julienne the same size as the taro root.

5. Cut out and discard the heavy stems from the collard leaves. Boil the leaves in a large pan of water for 1 minute, or until they are pliable but still a nice dark green. Drain and plunge into very cold water, then drain again and set aside.

6. Warm $1/2$ teaspoon of the oil in a large frying pan over medium-high heat. Sauté the Canadian bacon and green onions for 1 minute and remove to a large bowl.

7. Heat another $1/2$ teaspoon of oil in the same frying pan and add the taro strips. Spray lightly with cooking spray and sauté for 2 minutes. Sprinkle 2 tablespoons of the lime juice over the top

and add the pineapple strips. Continue cooking for another minute.

8. Transfer the taro and pineapple to the bowl with the Canadian bacon. Stir to combine and sprinkle with the crushed pepper flakes and the remaining $1\frac{1}{2}$ teaspoons of lime juice.

9. Preheat the oven to 350 degrees F [180 degrees C].

10. Warm the frying pan over high heat and add the remaining $\frac{1}{2}$ teaspoon of oil. Lay the tuna in the hot pan, dust with salt and pepper, and sear each side for 30 seconds. Remove to a plate.

To Assemble the Palusamis

11. Arrange the collard leaves, coconut cream, pineapple-taro filling, and tuna close at hand. You may have to play with the collard leaves a little to get them to wrap up into neat little packages. The trick I have found is to lay one leaf flat on the counter, its tip pointing at 12 o'clock. Lay two more leaves perpendicular to the first, their tips pointing to 3 o'clock and 9 o'clock and their bases meeting at the bottom of the first leaf. The leaves should form an upside-down T or three- pointed fan shape.

12. Spoon $\frac{1}{4}$ cup of the filling onto the center of the leaf arrangement. Top with a piece of tuna, another $\frac{1}{4}$ cup of filling, and 1 tablespoon of the chilled coconut cream. Fold the ends of the leaves over the filling into a little packet and secure with string. There is no set way to do this and a lot depends on the size of the collard leaves, so do what works for you. Repeat for the remaining 5 packages.

13. Lay the palusamis in a 9x13-inch [23x33-cm] baking dish. Cover loosely with foil and bake in the preheated oven for 20 minutes.

To Serve

14. Place one palusami on each warmed dinner plate. Remove the string and spoon some of the remaining coconut cream over

the top. Garnish with two tomato slices and serve a scoop of Green Bean Rice Pilau alongside.

Time Estimate
Hands-on, 45 minutes; unsupervised, 20 minutes.

Nutritional Profile per Serving
327 calories; 8 g fat; 3 g saturated fat; 22% of calories from fat; 34 g carbohydrate; 3 g dietary fiber.

Vegetarian Option: Plantain and Pineapple Wrapped in Greens
Warm the oil in a large frying pan over medium-high heat. Add the plantain, pineapple, onions, taro, salt, and chipotle sauce. Cook for 2 minutes, stirring to keep from burning. Pour the mixture into the center of a collard leaf or leaves, sprinkle the lime juice over the top, and add a dollop of the coconut cream. Wrap and tie as above. Serve with the remaining coconut cream.

Vegetarian Option Nutritional Profile per Serving
228 calories; 4 g fat; 1 g saturated fat; 14% of calories from fat; 49 g carbohydrate; 4 g dietary fiber.

Green Bean Rice Pilau

This dish represents the modern influence of Fiji, a relatively near neighbor that supplies the rice and Indian spices popular amongst the Samoan people.

SERVES 6

3 cups low-sodium chicken or vegetable stock
3 cardamom pods
1 cinnamon stick, 1½ inches [4 cm] long
⅛ teaspoon black peppercorns
¼ teaspoon ground turmeric
2 whole cloves
1 teaspoon light olive oil
1 cup finely diced onion
2 cloves garlic, peeled, bashed, and chopped
1 cup long-grain white rice
1 bay leaf
¼ teaspoon salt
1½ cups green beans, cut into ¼-inch [¾-cm] slices
¼ teaspoon ground cardamom
¼ cup raisins

1. Preheat the oven to 400 degrees F [205 degrees C].

2. Warm the stock in a small saucepan over medium-high heat. [Vegetarian Option: Use vegetable stock.] Pulverize the cardamom pods, cinnamon stick, peppercorns, turmeric, and cloves in a coffee mill or crush them with a mortar and pestle. Add the spice mixture to the stock and bring to a boil. Reduce the heat and simmer for about 30 minutes.

3. Heat ½ teaspoon of the oil in a medium ovenproof saucepan. Sauté the onion and garlic for 1 minute over medium heat. Add the rice and continue to cook for an additional 3 minutes.

4. Pour the seasoned stock through a strainer into the pan with the rice. Add the bay leaf and ⅛ teaspoon of the salt. Stir well and place, uncovered, in the preheated oven. Bake for

20 minutes, or until the rice is tender and the liquid is absorbed.

5. Heat the remaining $^1/_2$ teaspoon of oil in a large sauté pan. Add the green beans, remaining $^1/_8$ teaspoon of salt, and ground cardamom. Cook for 6 to 8 minutes, or until tender. You may need to add just a little water so the beans won't brown, but don't let them lose their bright green color.

6. After the rice has finished baking, stir in the green beans and raisins and serve immediately.

Time Estimate
Hands-on, 20 minutes; unsupervised, 50 minutes.

Nutritional Profile per Serving
172 calories; 2 g fat; 0 g saturated fat; 10% of calories from fat; 36 g carbohydrate; 2 g dietary fiber.

Koko Tapioca with Bananas and Crystallized Ginger

This dessert features humble tapioca blended with chocolate and bananas, two tastes that I found to be island favorites. Treena and I learned that it was Robert Louis Stevenson's wife who first introduced cocoa to the Samoan Islands. Now, it is a productive crop, second only to coconuts. For chocolate lovers, this creamy, luscious pudding will do the trick—Pacific style!

SERVES 6

> 1/2 cup small pearl tapioca
> 1/4 cup firmly packed brown sugar
> 1/4 cup Dutch-process or European-style cocoa
> 2 cups 2% milk
> 1/4 cup egg substitute
> 1/2 teaspoon vanilla extract
> 1/4 cup finely chopped crystallized ginger
> 3 ripe bananas

Garnish
> 2 tablespoons toasted almond slices

1. Soak the tapioca in 3 cups of water for 1 hour. Drain and set aside.

2. Combine the sugar and cocoa in the top of a double boiler over hot water. When they are well mixed, add 1/3 cup of boiling water and whisk until smooth.

3. Add the milk and cook over medium heat until the temperature reaches 140 degrees F [60 degrees C]. Cook for 5 minutes more, not letting the temperature rise above 155 degrees [65 degrees C].

4. Whisk in the drained tapioca and the egg substitute. Turn up the heat and cook over boiling water, stirring often, until the tapioca is tender and the pudding is thick, about 15 minutes.

5. Stir in the vanilla and ginger. Remove the pudding from the heat and set aside to cool.

6. Peel and slice the bananas and layer with the tapioca in six wine glasses or champagne flutes that hold about 1 cup each. Sprinkle the tops with almonds. This dessert may be served either chilled or at room temperature.

Time Estimate
Hands-on, 30 minutes; unsupervised, 1 hour.

Nutritional Profile per Serving
206 calories; 3 g fat; 1 g saturated fat; 13% of calories from fat; 42 g carbohydrate; 2 g dietary fiber.

Portability
The tapioca can be prepared ahead and carried in a plastic container. You may want to bring glasses for serving. Slice and add the bananas just before serving.

appetizer
Kokoda
Marinated white fish bright with the tastes of jalapeño, dill, and ginger, with a hint of coconut cream.

main course
Curried Chicken, Sweet Potatoes, and Bananas Wakaya
Sweet curry, set against the tartness of a tamarind sauce.

vegetarian option
Tofu and Bananas Wakaya

dessert
Fiji Fruit Baskets
Feather-light brandy snaps form a cup for fresh fruit and creamy yogurt.

travelogue

*T*he distance from American Samoa to Fiji is only about eight hundred miles, but we crossed the International Dateline on the way, thoroughly confusing my watch. We landed in the port of Suva on the island of Viti Levu, one of over three hundred islands that make up the country of Fiji. Early explorers called these the Cannibal Islands, and Captain Cook heard about them from the Tongas, who reported that the people there "were very fierce, always at war, possessed great weapons, great canoes, ate their captives, were famed warriors."

There was nothing fierce about the Fijians who met us at the pier, although they could be classified as warriors. Fiji maintains a notable militia, and one of their military bands turned out to greet our ship in style, with uniforms sparkling and brass instruments flashing. Their precision marching reminded me of my own military days and was clearly a relic of the British, who controlled these islands from 1874 until 1970.

Another legacy from the English is the ethnic makeup of the islands. When Great Britain introduced sugarcane plantations to

Love of Land and Connection to Community

Fiji

Previous page:
I film taro root moving into the market.

This page, from top:
A marching band turns out for our arrival.

The market in Suva comes in two layers, each equally delectable.

Tupou Moefo, our indefatigable guide, charms and hosts us in style.

Fiji in the 1800s, they imported large numbers of indentured laborers from India to work the fields and harvest the cane. Today almost half the population is Indian, or Indo-Fijian, as they are called. Although the native Fijians and Indo-Fijians have lived together for almost a century, the two groups rarely intermarry, and their customs and religions have remained quite distinct. For the most part the two cultures have lived harmoniously, but in recent years tension has arisen over issues of land ownership.

There were walls of green and white bok choy, tables filled with Scotch Bonnet peppers and fresh gingerroot, side by side, as though they knew they are meant for one another.

Native Fijians still live in an agricultural society and feel a very deep-seated personal bond with their family lands. Meet a Fijian and they will look you directly in the eye, proud of who they are and the land beneath their feet. They do lease out certain portions of acreage, but for only ten years at a time. Indo-Fijian farmers regard this system as unfair and feel they need longer leases to justify their investments in making the land productive.

"So," you may be asking, "what does this have to do with my dinner?" Well, for one thing, it explains why there are two very different and very interesting cuisines in Fiji. It also explains why so many of the "old ways" of traditional Polynesian culture survive in Fiji despite a century of outside influence.

And it explains some of the unusual items for sale at the food market in Suva. This marvelous market is housed in a large two-story building, and the bottom floor is loaded with fresh food—vegetables, seafood, fruit, and all manner of fabulous things to eat. There were walls of green and white bok choy, tables filled with Scotch Bonnet peppers and fresh gingerroot, side by side, as though they knew they are meant for one another. Upstairs on the second floor, the Indo-Fijian rules the roost with sack after sack brimming with spices and pungent herbs. Here are the dried foods, the cinnamon, cumin seed, fenugreek, and great mounds of cardamom seeds tightly enclosed in their shells. A huge pile of star anise caught my eye and the need for a tamarind-flavored curry became extreme!

Lunch, however, was over a hundred and eighty miles away. Accompanied by our host Tupou Moefo, a handsome Fijian rugby player, we headed out to Nadi international airport through lush green fields. We noticed curious patches of green on the dry slopes of the nearby mountains, and Tupou explained that these were plots of cassava, a tall plant that forms a large tuberous root, also known as manioc and in Fiji, as *tavioka*. They are the source of little pearl-like beads called tapioca. Cassava is a staple food of indigenous peoples throughout the tropics. Sometimes the brown roots are boiled, then peeled and eaten whole. Sometimes the cooked roots are beaten into a paste and made into a sort of bread called *madrai ni viti*, or Fijian bread. When I wondered at the use of the word *viti*, Tupou said that was the Fijian word for their homeland, mispronounced by Europeans as Fiji.

We flew out of Nadi and landed on a small green dot in the middle of the big blue sea. The island of Wakaya is three thousand acres of paradise. Imagine huge old mango trees, a green-turfed golf course, and a white coral beach. Now conjure the sound of a quiet sea lapping the beach and the rustle of cooling palm fronds. Then imagine a herd of reindeer, yes reindeer, grazing beneath the

This page, from top:
Wakaya, seen from above: an island paradise.
We tour the herb gardens with Lynda Miller.
A cool breeze and iced tea beckon.

Imagine huge old mango trees, a green-turfed golf course, and a white coral beach. Now conjure the sound of a quiet sea lapping the beach and the rustle of cooling palm fronds.

mango trees. The experience was enough to send me to my hut. My "hut" was beautifully crafted of native wood, using traditional architecture and building methods. From the porch I could see the organic gardens maintained by Lynda Miller, who helps her husband manage this small resort. They have room for only eight guests at a time, making this a perfect respite from the modern world. Produce from Lynda's garden goes straight to the kitchen and into the great food served in their dining room. Treena and I were ready to stay and eat their cooking for several days, but Tupou reminded us that we had a boat to catch.

As our little airplane climbed into the sky to return us to Nadi, I thought of Santa Claus and his reindeer. Perhaps the old guy isn't

travelogue 🐢 II. FIJI

working away under the ice at the North Pole after all; he's swinging in a hammock on a secluded beach.

This dinner reflects the two cuisines of Fiji. The first course is the Fijian version of ceviche, drenched in fresh lime juice and then bound together with coconut cream. For an entrée, I cooked up an Indo-Fijian curry full of chicken, banana, and sweet potato. The dessert is a cookie basket made of ginger, sugar, and imagine: butter! The basket is filled with tropical fruit macerated in tonic water and lime zest. You can enjoy this entire menu for only about 900 calories, with 17% of the calories from fat. The vegetarian option is only 828 calories and 15% of calories from fat.

Kokoda

Pickling is an ancient way to preserve fresh fish without refrigeration. The technique may be found in a number of cultures around the world and has practical, as well as delicious, benefits. In this Fijian version of ceviche, the raw fish is marinated in lime juice and turns perfectly white. The fresh combination of seasonings, colors, and textures makes this a splendid appetizer. I've adjusted the coconut cream to provide minimal saturated fat while retaining the essential flavors and textures that are so important to this dish.

SERVES 6

6	ounces [168 g] orange roughy* fillet
1/2	cup plus 1 tablespoon fresh lime juice
1/2	cup finely chopped sweet onion
1	jalapeño pepper, cored, seeded, and very finely diced
1	small tomato, cored, seeded, and finely diced
1/2	red bell pepper, cored, seeded, and finely diced
1	piece of English cucumber, about 3 inches [8-cm] skin scored with a fork, finely diced
1/4	cup diced hearts of palm*
1	tablespoon chopped fresh dill weed
1/2	teaspoon very finely diced fresh gingerroot
12	medium shrimp [about 1 1/2 ounces or 42 g each], peeled and deveined
1/16	teaspoon salt
1/16	teaspoon freshly ground black pepper
3/4	cup coconut cream [page 160]

Garnish
6 sprigs fresh dill weed

Vegetarian Option [per Serving]
1 cup diced hearts of palm

1. Cut the fish into 1-inch [2 1/2 -cm] pieces and place in a small bowl. Cover with 1/2 cup of the lime juice and soak for 1 hour.

2. Combine the onion, jalapeño, tomato, red pepper, cucumber,

*Orange Roughy

This small saltwater fish is imported from New Zealand and only recently began appearing in my supermarket, usually in frozen form. The fillets are pure white with a delicate flavor; flounder, cod, or sole would be fine substitutes.

*Hearts of Palm

These are the tender inside layers of the palmetto palm, which grows in tropical climates. The thick white cylinders will remind you of artichoke hearts, and I have found them to be tremendously versatile as a low-fat option in a number of salads and other dishes. You'll find them canned in jars at any good supermarket.

hearts of palm, dill, and ginger in a large bowl. [Vegetarian Option: Set aside one-sixth of this mixture per vegetarian serving before proceeding].

3. Heat the remaining 1 tablespoon of lime juice in a medium frying pan. Add the shrimp, season with the salt and pepper, and cook for about 1½ minutes, or until the shrimp are bright pink. Remove from the pan and cut each shrimp into 4 pieces. Add the chopped shrimp to the bowl of vegetables. Drain the fish and add to the bowl.

4. Add the coconut cream and stir gently until the fish and vegetables are lightly coated.

5. Serve on salad plates garnished with sprigs of fresh dill.

Time Estimate
Hands-on, 25 minutes; unsupervised, 1 hour.

Nutritional Profile per Serving
159 calories; 3 g fat; 1 g saturated fat; 20% of calories from fat; 12 g carbohydrate; 1 g dietary fiber.

Vegetarian Option
Add the diced hearts of palm to the reserved vegetable mixture. Coat with coconut cream and garnish with dill.

Vegetarian Option Nutritional Profile per Serving
168 calories; 1 g fat; 1 g saturated fat; 7% of calories from fat; 39 g carbohydrate; 3 g dietary fiber.

Portability
Prepare the dish through Step 3 just before you leave home so the vegetables will remain nice and fresh. Stir in the coconut cream when you are ready to serve. Wrap the dill sprigs in a damp paper towel in the bottom of a plastic container.

Curried Chicken, Sweet Potatoes, and Bananas Wakaya

This delicious curry comes from the Indo-Fijian population of the islands, while the sauce captures the intriguing, mysterious flavor of the tamarind. To me, the sweet and sour taste sensations contained within the tamarind fruit capture the zest of the island of Wakaya. If you have trouble finding tamarind pods to make the sauce, you can substitute a good mango chutney and add a little fresh lemon juice. I know the preparation for this dish appears to be complicated, but the actual labor is quite light. An unusual, attractive curry...and easy to make!

SERVES 6

Tamarind Sauce

- 1¹/₂ ounces [42 g] or about 15 inches [38 cm] peeled tamarind pods
- 1 teaspoon light olive oil
- ¹/₄ teaspoon yellow mustard seeds
- 1 teaspoon cumin seeds
- ¹/₄ teaspoon garam masala*
- ¹/₈ teaspoon cayenne pepper [optional]
- 5 quarter-size slices fresh gingerroot
- 3 ounces [84 g] pitted dates [about 12]
- 1 mango, peeled and cubed

Chicken

- ³/₄ teaspoon India Ethmix [*page* 128] or good Madras curry powder
- 3 boneless chicken breasts, skin on, about 6 ounces [168 g] each
- 2 teaspoons light olive oil

Curry

- 2 heads bok choy [*page* 147]
- 3 bananas
- ¹/₃ cup fresh lemon juice
- 12 ounces [340 g] steamed sweet potato, peeled, halved and cut into 1-inch [2¹/₂-cm] pieces

*Garam Masala

Garam masala is an Indian spice mixture usually added at the end of cooking. It is composed of cinnamon, cardamom, cloves, cumin and other "warming" spices. If you can't find a good variety at your market, try this combination:

- 1 piece cinnamon, about 2-inches [5-cm] long
- 6 allspice berries
- ¹/₄ teaspoon nutmeg
- 4 whole cloves

Blend to a powder in a small electric coffee grinder designated for this purpose. Shake through a sieve and store in a small jar.

<pre>
  1 teaspoon arrowroot
 1/2 cup low-sodium chicken or vegetable stock
  2 cloves garlic, peeled, bashed, and chopped
  2 teaspoons India Ethmix [page 128] or good Madras
     curry powder
 1/2 cup yogurt cheese [page 37]
  4 green onions, white and green parts, cut into 1/4-inch
     [3/4-cm] slices
</pre>

Garnish

<pre>
  1 mango, peeled and sliced
 1/2 English cucumber, unpeeled, cut into very thin strips
 12 small radishes
</pre>

Vegetarian Option [per Serving]

<pre>
  4 ounces [112 g] extra-firm light tofu
 1/2 teaspoon light olive oil
 1/4 teaspoon India Ethmix or good Madras curry powder
 1/4 cup low-sodium vegetable stock
</pre>

To Prepare the Tamarind Sauce

1. Cut the peeled tamarind pods into small pieces and soak in 1/2 cup of warm water for 15 minutes. Strain, reserving the liquid and pulp, and discard the seeds.

2. Warm the oil in a small frying pan over medium-high heat. Add the mustard and cumin seeds and cook for 2 minutes. Transfer to a blender or food processor.

3. Add the garam masala, optional cayenne pepper, ginger, and the reserved tamarind pulp and liquid. Process at high speed for 1 minute. Add the dates and mango and continue blending for another minute. Press the sauce through a strainer with a purée press or large spoon. Set aside until ready to use.

To Prepare the Chicken

4. Rub 1/2 teaspoon of the India Ethmix or curry powder into the skinless side of each of the chicken breasts.

5. Warm the oil in a large frying pan over medium-high heat. Sauté the breasts, skin side down, for 2 minutes. Turn the

breasts and cook for another 3 minutes. Turn twice more, cooking for a total of 9 minutes, or until just cooked through. Remove from the pan and set aside. Do not wash the pan.

To Prepare the Curry

6. Cut the leaves off the bok choy stems and wash well. Steam the leaves for 1 minute and cool immediately under cold running water. Drain well and pat dry; set aside to use as a bed for the curry.

7. Cut off and discard the tough bottoms of the bok choy stems. Slice the tender parts of the stems into $1/2$-inch [$1^1/2$-cm] strips. Set aside for the garnish.

8. Peel the bananas and cut into 1-inch [$2^1/2$-cm] pieces. Coat the pieces with the lemon juice in a large bowl to keep them from turning brown. Gently toss the sweet potato pieces with the bananas and transfer to a large steamer. Cover and steam for 5 minutes to heat through. [Vegetarian Option: Set aside one-sixth of this mixture per serving before proceeding to the next step.]

9. Combine the arrowroot with the stock to make a slurry.

10. Reheat the oil and chicken cooking juices remaining in the large frying pan. Add the garlic and India Ethmix and stir just long enough to heat through. Deglaze the pan with the arrowroot slurry, loosening the flavorful bits from the bottom.

11. Spoon the yogurt cheese into a 2-cup glass measure. Add a little of the hot stock and mix well to temper the yogurt. Whisk in the rest of the stock to make a smooth, creamy sauce.

12. Combine the curry sauce with the hot bananas and sweet potatoes in a high-sided skillet. Keep warm but do not boil.

13. Remove and discard the skin from the chicken and cut the meat into 1-inch [$2^1/2$-cm] pieces. Gently stir the chicken and onions into the banana mixture over medium-high heat.

To Serve

14. Arrange two or three bok choy leaves on each dinner plate.

Place a serving of the curry on the bok choy leaves and garnish with the bok choy strips, mango slices, cucumber strips, and radishes. Spoon a dollop of tamarind sauce or mango chutney on the side as a condiment.

Time Estimate
Hands-on, 50 minutes; unsupervised, 15 minutes.

Nutritional Profile per Serving
465 calories; 7 g fat; 1 g saturated fat; 14% of calories from fat; 68 g carbohydrate; 8 g dietary fiber.

Vegetarian Option: Tofu and Bananas Wakaya
Cut the tofu into 1-inch [2½-cm] cubes and dry with a paper towel. Warm the oil in a frying pan over medium heat. Add the tofu and sprinkle with the India Ethmix. Pour 1 tablespoon of the tamarind sauce or chutney over the tofu and cook for 2 minutes. Add the vegetable stock and simmer until reduced to a thick syrup. Combine with the reserved bananas and sweet potatoes. Garnish.

Vegetarian Option Nutritional Profile per Serving
380 calories; 6 g fat; 1 g saturated fat; 14% of calories from fat; 70 g carbohydrate; 8 g dietary fiber.

Fiji Fruit Baskets

Old-fashioned brandy snaps are a wonderful way to end a spicy meal, but they are traditionally full of butter and sugar. However, thanks to Susan Purdy, our good low-fat baking friend, you can now make a crisp, buttery ginger snap. As a special treat, we shape the cookies into cups in which to serve a delicious tropical fruit salad. You can also make small cookies from this recipe whenever you have a craving for fresh ginger snaps. They're perhaps a bit too irresistible.

SERVES 6

Fruit Salad

- 1/2 fresh pineapple, peeled, cored, and cut into 1/2-inch [1 1/2-cm] dice
- 2 bananas, peeled and cut into 1/2-inch [1 1/2-cm] dice
- 1 mango, peeled, seeded, and cut into 1/2-inch [1 1/2-cm] dice
- 1 teaspoon finely grated lime zest
- 1 1/2 cups tonic water

Cookie Cups

- 1/4 cup packed dark brown sugar
- 1/4 cup dark corn syrup
- 2 teaspoons unsulfered molasses*
- 2 tablespoons butter
- 2 tablespoons light olive oil
- 1/4 cup unsweetened apple juice
- 1/2 teaspoon ground ginger
- 1/4 teaspoon ground cinnamon
- 2/3 cup sifted all-purpose flour

Cream Filling

- 1 1/4 cups low-fat vanilla yogurt

To Prepare the Salad

1. Combine the diced pineapple, bananas, and mango in a glass bowl. Sprinkle with the lime zest and cover with tonic water. Refrigerate until you are ready to use, but no longer than overnight.

*Unsulfured Molasses

Light molasses comes from the first boiling of the juices, dark molasses from the second, and blackstrap molasses from the last. Sulfur dioxide is sometimes used to lighten the syrup, but it leaves an unpleasant aftertaste. I recommend unsulfured molasses; the label will say if sulfur has been used.

To Prepare the Cookie Cups

2. Preheat the oven to 400 degrees F [205 degrees C]. Coat three or four cookie sheets with cooking spray.

3. Set out four to six small juice glasses, large spice jars, or other cylindrical objects about 1 3/4 inches [4 1/2 cm] in diameter and at least 3 inches [8 cm] tall. You will use these to shape the warm cookies. [You don't really need all six because you can only bake two cookies at a time and they cool quite quickly.]

4. In a large saucepan, combine the sugar, corn syrup, molasses, butter, oil, apple juice, ginger, and cinnamon. Bring to a boil over medium-high heat, stirring constantly, and boil vigorously for 1 minute. Remove from the heat and stir in the flour with a wire whisk. Beat until smooth.

5. Drop 1 tablespoon of the batter in a puddle on each half of a greased cookie sheet. [You will only be able to cook two cookies per sheet.] Using the back of a spoon, spread the batter into two smooth, thin circles 5 1/4 inches [14 cm] in diameter. Make sure there is plenty of space between the circles.

6. Bake for 7 to 8 minutes, or until the cookies are a dark golden brown. Watch carefully as they will burn easily. I set my timer for 5 minutes and add time depending on their color. Set the baking sheet on a wire rack and allow the wafers to cool for about 2 minutes.

7. Use a metal spatula to loosen and lift the wafers and drape them atop the inverted glasses. This is the tricky part. If the wafers are too hot, they will tear. If they are too cool, they won't form into cups. As you start loosening around the edges, you will be able to tell if they are ready. If they get too cool, you can reheat them in the oven. There is enough batter to make at least 10 cups, so you can do a little experimenting. The bent and broken bits make splendid snacks.

8. As the cookies firm up [this will happen very quickly], set them on a wire rack to cool completely. If the batter should get too thick to work easily, just rewarm it on the stove. When

completely cool, the cups can be carefully stored in an airtight
container, where they will keep up to a week.

To Serve

9. Drain the fruit in a colander and discard the juice—or drink
   it. Stir the yogurt with a spoon to liquefy it and spoon about
   2 tablespoons into each cookie cup. Divide the fruit among the
   cups and top with a dollop of yogurt.

Time Estimate

Hands-on, 1 hour.

Nutritional Profile per Serving

280 calories; 7 g fat; 2 g saturated fat; 23% of calories from fat;
54 g carbohydrate; 2 g dietary fiber.

Portability

The cups can be made up to a week beforehand and stored in an
airtight container. A large, rigid container works well for both
storage and transport. The fruit can be macerated [soaked in the
tonic water] and drained at home and carried in a resealable bag.
The yogurt can be transported and stirred in its original container.
This dessert goes together very quickly when all the parts
are ready.

Note:

To make small cookies instead of cups, drop the batter by
teaspoonfuls several inches apart. Using the back of a spoon,
spread the batter into thin rounds and bake as above.

appetizer
Pickled Green-Lipped Mussels
Colorful New Zealand mussels pickled in a light rice vinegar and served on crisp Belgian endive spears.

main course
Venison Canterbury
Boneless leg of venison in a "hedgerow" seasoning of blackberry and orange sauce.

vegetarian option
Browned Eggplant Canterbury

vegetables
Mashed Sweet Potatoes
Sweet and creamy and touched with thyme.

Steamed Spinach with Nutmeg
Flavorful, loaded with vitamins, and brightened with fresh nutmeg.

dessert
Promised Land Meringue Cake
Delicate meringue shell filled with fresh fruit in a spectacular presentation.

travelogue

*A*s we headed south from Fiji toward the twin islands of New Zealand, Treena and I were feeling that our trip had, indeed, been a journey of discovery. We had made many new friends and tasted many new foods, and we had also enjoyed a surprising number of homecomings and reunions with people and places of our past. Our arrival in Auckland was another reminder of a special part of our personal history. I first came to New Zealand in the 1950s as a young military officer, serving as the chief catering advisor for the New Zealand Air Force. My early days in television took place in New Zealand and I met many people on this stop who recollected my first radio show, "The Cook's Tour" on "Woman's Hour."

Our return to New Zealand also reminded us of a contentious dispute that continues to this day and involves a great deal of

NEW ZEALAND
Fruit and Honey in the Promised Land

passion, intrigue, politics, and emotion. No, it is not a civil war. It is the great marmite vs. vegemite debate. For anyone who doesn't know, marmite and vegemite are yeast extracts that are very

I met many people in New Zealand who recollected my first radio show, "The Cook's Tour."

popular in Australia and New Zealand, though quite obscure in the rest of the world. Both are dark brown salty pastes that are spread on sandwiches, toast, muffins, and many other things as well. Both are habit-forming, judging from the quantities shipped to expatriate Kiwis [New Zealanders] in food parcels from home. Both contain yeast extract, salt, artificial colors, and vitamins. The argument stems from which tastes better. Most New Zealanders prefer marmite, while Australians tend to go for vegemite. After much thought and a close look at the two labels, I believe I know why New Zealanders choose marmite: sugar is its second ingredient.

Having laid that debate to rest, let's address another gastronomic controversy which has swirled between the two nations for over fifty years. This dispute began with the visit of the famous ballerina Pavlova to Perth, Australia in July of 1929, when she captivated the town with her performances. Five years later, in 1934, Mrs. Elizabeth Paxton, manager of the Esplanade Hotel, asked her chef to devise some new delicacies to add pizzazz to afternoon tea at the hotel. The chef concocted a soft-centered meringue cake filled with whipped cream and fresh fruit and presented it to his boss, who remarked, "It's as light as Pavlova!" Soon everyone in the country wanted a piece of Pavlova, the new Australian creation. But when word filtered across the Tasman Sea to New Zealand, the plot thickened. There was nothing new about that dessert, the Kiwis cried. They'd been making it for years. Documentation is on the side of the Kiwis. A 1929 cookbook published in New Zealand contains a recipe for Pavlova Cakes in the form of three dozen little meringues. [This cook apparently chose to honor the Corps de Ballet as well as the prima ballerina.] Meringue cakes were popular items in New Zealand in the 1930s, and food sleuths hypothesize that the Esplanade chef saw a prize-winning recipe for such a cake in an issue of *Women's Mirror* magazine, added some cornstarch, and...Pavlova!

Well, there you have it. History, even that of food, is a tangled web. The history of New Zealand itself is also full of twists and turns. According to ancient legend, a Polynesian fisherman belonging to a tribe called Maori was out fishing one day when an octopus swallowed his bait. The fisherman set off in pursuit of the octopus, and soon found himself far from land. After sailing for many days, he spied an island on the horizon and named it *Aotearoa*, Land of the Long White Cloud. Navigating by the stars, he returned to his homeland and told his people of the island. Several hundred years later, around 1350 A.D., the Maoris retraced his journey in large canoes equipped with sails and outriggers. Like the ancient

There is tremendous potential in the foods of New Zealand, and I have gathered several of them in this menu for you to enjoy.

Hawaiians, they carried dried fruit, seeds, root vegetables, and dogs. The climate was cooler than in their previous home, and the bananas and coconuts they planted did not do well, but the taro and sweet potatoes did. They lived near the coast, hunting whales and seals and shellfish as well as moas, huge flightless birds that are now extinct. They launched their long canoes to do battle with other tribes, but for the most part they lived in relative isolation until 1642, when the Dutch explorer Abel Tasman dropped anchor and sent a small exploring party ashore. The party was promptly killed and eaten. I should explain that the Maoris believed that if you ate your enemy you would absorb his power. This was clearly before we began to learn about saturated fats, and at that time five-a-day might have been misunderstood.

Britain colonized New Zealand in the 1830s, signing a treaty with the Maoris that promised them protection and possession of their lands. But floods of white settlers and various injustices led to years of chaos, which finally seem to be coming close to resolution. Although the Maoris are now a minority of the population, they have preserved important elements of their culture. Maori history has been handed down in carvings, stories, and songs. Their music is moving and beautiful and a visit to a Maori village during a *hui* [gathering] is a special experience. Their feasts include meat and vegetables steamed in a *hangi* [earth oven] and a porridge made from fermented corn.

Apart from the traditional Maori foods and the beloved marmite and Pavlova, there are very few dishes unique to New Zealand. Many culinary professionals are working to change that, using

This page, from top:
Palms swaying in the breeze are a cruise theme.
Pip Duncan, one of our favorite "food people."
Hamming it up on-air brings back memories of my early days in New Zealand radio.

the islands' wonderful seasonal produce and fresh seafood as a base. I sought out several of these "food people," such as Pip Duncan, Brendon Turner, Lea Stenig, and the talented Chef Tony Smith of the Park Royal Hotel in Christchurch. They all generously shared their time and talents with us in discussing ways to make the most of indigenous ingredients.

There is tremendous potential in the foods of New Zealand, and I have gathered several of them in this menu for you to enjoy with your friends. New Zealand Green-Lipped Mussels will set an exotic tone, followed by medallions of grassfed venison, an exciting food of the future that is low in fat, full of flavor, and free of artificial hormones. The venison is complemented by nutmeg-flavored leaf spinach and brilliant orange mashed sweet potatoes. Dessert simply had to be Pavlova, but when I stepped back and admired its filling of fruit and honey, I decided to call it Promised Land Meringue Cake. This meal has 715 calories with 13% of calories from fat. An especially good example of low-fat vegetarian options is the use of eggplant slices in place of venison; the vegetarian meal comes to 577 calories and 6 grams of fat, almost all unsaturated.

Pickled Green-Lipped Mussels

New Zealand Green-Lipped Mussels are large and succulent and unique. They often sport bright orange flesh with delicate green-edged shells—definitely the fashion plates of the shellfish world. I chose to pickle them in a light rice vinegar for this delectable appetizer, served on crisp Belgian endive spears with good dark rye bread. This pickling method is quite versatile and can be used for other fish and shellfish. The poaching liquid works nicely for a quick bowl of steamed mussels anytime you see them fresh or frozen on the half shell in your market.

SERVES 6

Court Bouillon [Poaching Liquid]

- 1/2 teaspoon light olive oil
- 1 medium sweet onion, finely chopped
- 4 cloves garlic, peeled, bashed, and chopped
- 1 tablespoon dried basil
- 4 cups dry white wine [I prefer dealcoholized Ariel Chardonnay]*
- 2 bay leaves
- 3 broad sprigs fresh parsley, bashed
- 1 teaspoon salt
- 1/2 lemon

Mussels

- 2 dozen New Zealand Green-Lipped Mussels* or 3 dozen blue mussels, fresh or frozen

Pickling Liquid

- 1/2 lemon, thinly sliced
- 1 cup rice vinegar
- 1 bay leaf
- 1 teaspoon whole cloves
- 1 teaspoon whole allspice
- 1/2 red bell pepper, cored, seeded, and cut into thin strips
- 2 sprigs fresh dill weed

*Ariel Chardonnay

I like to use dealcoholized wine in my recipes, and I prefer the Ariel label because the folks there produce classic, finely crafted wines that have had the alcohol removed by a cold centrifuge process. I've used Ariel chardonnay in this recipe for mussels because it imparts the mellow flavor of chardonnay grapes without the bitterness of alcohol.

*Green-Lipped Mussels

Green-Lipped Mussels are sometimes available fresh. They're always available frozen, if you will ask your fishmonger to order them. You can certainly substitute our more common blue mussels, but you'll need more of them.

*Belgian Endive

This handsome member of the chicory family is slightly bitter and arrives in a small, tightly packed head, like tiny romaine. It is grown in the dark, so it is pale yellow or white and is wonderful mixed with mild greens or served with appetizers.

Garnish

Belgian endive*

12 slices dark rye cocktail bread

Vegetarian Option [per Serving]

1 large or 2 small artichoke hearts

To Prepare the Court Bouillon

1. Warm the oil in a large frying pan over medium heat. Sauté the onion, garlic, and basil for 2 minutes, or until softened. Add the wine, bay leaves, parsley, and salt. Squeeze the lemon juice into the pan and add the rind as well. Simmer for 10 minutes.

2. Strain the bouillon, returning the liquid to the frying pan and discarding the seasonings.

To Cook the Mussels

3. Scrub and debeard the mussels, discarding any that are no longer alive. If you have bought mussels frozen on the half shell, this step isn't necessary.

4. Bring the court bouillon to a boil and add the mussels. Cover the pan and poach for 3 minutes. Strain, reserving 4 cups of the liquid. Scoop the meat out of the shells into a small bowl. Carefully wash the shells and remove the "foot" from the inside. Set the shells aside to use at serving time.

To Prepare the Pickling Liquid

5. Add the lemon slices to the reserved court bouillon. Stir in the rice vinegar, bay leaf, cloves, allspice berries, and red pepper strips.

6. Place the mussels in a jar and cover with the seasoned pickling liquid. Top with the dill. Cover and store in the refrigerator overnight, or up to 3 days. This is a light pickle not suited to storage.

To Serve

7. Place four mussel shells on each plate. Lay an endive leaf in

each shell and top with mussels and pepper strips. Serve the bread on the side.

Time Estimate
Hands-on, 35 minutes; unsupervised, overnight.

Nutritional Profile per Serving
179 calories; 3 g fat; 1 g saturated fat; 18% of calories from fat; 21 g carbohydrate; 3 g dietary fiber.

Vegetarian Option
Replace the mussels with 4 marinated artichoke heart quarters, or halves if they are small.

Vegetarian Option Nutritional Profile per Serving
127 calories; 5 g fat; 0 g saturated fat; 33% of calories from fat; 20 g carbohydrate; 5 g dietary fiber.

Portability
Carry the pickled mussels and pepper strips to the party in their liquid, or drain and transfer them to a resealable bag. Separate the endive spears and carry in a plastic storage container so they don't get bruised. And don't forget the bread.

Venison Canterbury

Herds of farm-raised New Zealand deer receive excellent care and produce flavorful, tender venison. I created a "hedgerow" sauce of blackberries and fresh herbs to bring out the slight herb taste in the venison. Serve with Mashed Sweet Potatoes [page 193] and Steamed Spinach with Nutmeg [page 194] for a delicious blend of great tastes.

SERVES 6

Blackberry Sauce

1	tablespoon honey
3/4	cup finely sliced shallots [about 3 medium cloves]
1	tablespoon freshly grated gingerroot
1/2	cup plus 2 tablespoons orange juice
2 1/2	cups blackberries, fresh or frozen
1	tablespoon balsamic vinegar
2	fresh sage leaves
1	sprig fresh thyme, about 3 inches [8 cm] long
1	tablespoon arrowroot
1/2	cup low-sodium beef or vegetable stock

Venison

1/4	teaspoon salt
1	teaspoon freshly ground black pepper
1/2	teaspoon rubbed sage
1/2	teaspoon dried thyme
1 1/2	pounds [675 g] boneless leg of venison, cut into 12 medallions
1	teaspoon light olive oil

Vegetarian Option [per Serving]

1	teaspoon light olive oil
3	thick slices eggplant

1. Preheat the oven to 350 degrees F [180 degrees C].

To Prepare the Sauce

2. Bring the honey to a boil in a small saucepan over medium-high heat. When it is thick and bubbling, add the

shallots and ginger. Cook for a few minutes, stirring frequently, until the shallots are soft and lightly browned.

3. As the sauce thickens, add $1/2$ cup of the orange juice, a little at a time. When you have about a quarter of a cup of orange juice left, pour it in all at once. Stir in the blackberries, balsamic vinegar, sage leaves, and thyme sprig. Simmer gently for 3 or 4 minutes, or until the berries are heated through and give up their juice.

4. Pour the sauce through a fine strainer set over a small saucepan. Press with a purée press or the back of a spoon, discarding the seeds and pulp. You should have about 1 cup of juice.

5. Mix the arrowroot with the remaining 2 tablespoons of orange juice to make a slurry. Add the slurry and the stock to the blackberry juice and set aside without heating while you cook the meat. [Vegetarian Option: Use vegetable stock here and set aside $1/4$ cup of sauce per vegetarian serving before proceeding to the next step.]

To Prepare the Venison

6. Measure the salt, pepper, sage, and thyme into a large paper or plastic bag. Add the venison medallions and shake to coat.

7. Heat the oil in a large ovenproof frying pan. When the pan is very hot, brown the venison medallions for 1 minute. Turn and brown the other side for 1 minute. Bake in the preheated oven for 4 minutes while you finish the sauce.

8. Warm the sauce over medium heat, stirring frequently, until thickened and clear. Pour over the venison, stirring to capture the flavorful bits on the bottom of the frying pan.

To Serve

9. Place two medallions of venison on each warmed dinner plate and spoon any extra sauce over the meat. Arrange portions of Mashed Sweet Potatoes and Steamed Spinach on the side.

Time Estimate
Hands-on, 40 minutes.

Nutritional Profile per Serving
202 calories; 6 g fat; 3 g saturated fat; 25% of calories from fat;
13 g carbohydrate; 0 g dietary fiber.

Vegetarian Option: Browned Eggplant Canterbury
Warm the oil in a medium skillet over medium-high heat. Cook
the eggplant slices for 2 or 3 minutes per side, or until browned
and tender. Spoon the reserved blackberry sauce over the top.

Vegetarian Option Nutritional Profile per Serving
116 calories; 4 g fat; 1 g saturated fat; 33% of calories from fat;
20 g carbohydrate; 5 g dietary fiber.

Mashed Sweet Potatoes

The sweet potato is a favorite food in New Zealand, where it is called the kumera and is often smaller and slightly sweeter than our typical varieties. Married with a little fresh thyme, it makes a perfect side dish for the venison. You'll notice that this is not intended to be a purée, but a roughly mashed dish with plenty of texture.

SERVES 6

1³/₄ pounds [785 g] sweet potatoes, peeled and cut into
¹/₄-inch [³/₄-cm] slices
2 teaspoons fresh thyme leaves
¹/₈ teaspoon salt
¹/₈ teaspoon white pepper

1. Place the sweet potato slices in a vegetable steamer, cover, and steam for 16 minutes, or until soft. Transfer the potatoes to a medium bowl and roughly mash them with the thyme leaves. Season with the salt and white pepper.

2. To keep the potatoes warm, set the bowl over the top of a large saucepan that is partially filled with warm water. Cover the bowl and keep warm over low heat.

Time Estimate
Hands-on, 10 minutes; unsupervised, 16 minutes.

Nutritional Profile per Serving
137 calories; 0 g fat; 0 g saturated fat; 1% of calories from fat; 33 g carbohydrate; 4 g dietary fiber.

Steamed Spinach with Nutmeg

Something altogether splendid happens when you season spinach with nutmeg—just a touch does the trick. If it is available, use New Zealand spinach here—it's the kind with the flat leaves shaped like spades. A special bonus? It's full of nutrition.

SERVES 6

4	bunches fresh spinach, washed, stemmed, and drained
1/8	teaspoon salt
1/8	teaspoon freshly ground black pepper
1/8	teaspoon nutmeg

1. Place the spinach in a vegetable steamer and sprinkle with the salt, pepper, and nutmeg. Cover and steam for 3 minutes, or until the leaves are just limp but still bright green.

2. Thoroughly drain the spinach in a colander or sieve and keep warm until ready to serve.

Time Estimate
Hands-on, 15 minutes; unsupervised, 3 minutes.

Nutritional Profile per Serving
25 calories; 0 g fat; 0 g saturated fat; 11% of calories from fat; 4 g carbohydrate; 3 g dietary fiber.

Promised Land Meringue Cake

Although there is controversy over where it originated, Pavlova is certainly considered the national dessert of New Zealand. I set out to devise a new filling of fruit and honey to replace the whipped cream of the classic form, and by the time I was finished I felt like I had invented a whole new dessert, so I renamed it. The fruit wine sauce is a brand-new technique created especially for this dish, but it easily can be used elsewhere.

*Fireweed Honey

I don't know if fireweed grows in New Zealand, but it does grow wild through the northern United States and the southern parts of Canada, particularly along the Pacific coast. It makes my favorite honey, so I recommend it to you—authentic or not! Light in color, it has a delicate flavor that is quite versatile.

SERVES 6

Meringue Shell

- 5 large egg whites, at room temperature
- ²/₃ cup sugar
- 1 teaspoon vanilla extract
- 1 teaspoon distilled vinegar
- 2 teaspoons cornstarch

Fruit Wine Sauce

- 1 tablespoon honey*
- 2 nectarines, peeled, fruit reserved for filling
- 1 teaspoon lemon zest from ¹/₂ lemon
- ¹/₈ teaspoon ground cardamom
- 1 cup fruity white wine [I prefer dealcoholized Ariel Blanc]
- 2 teaspoons arrowroot
- 4 teaspoons water

Fruit Filling

- 2 kiwi fruit, peeled and sliced
- 2 nectarines, sliced
- 12 fresh strawberries, stemmed and sliced
  Other soft fruit or berries in season

To Prepare the Shell

1. Preheat the oven to 300 degrees F [150 degrees C]. Make sure the egg whites are at room temperature before beginning the recipe.

2. Cut a piece of baking parchment to fit a baking sheet. Draw a 9-inch [23-cm] circle on the parchment, turn it over, and place on top of the baking sheet.

3. Make sure that the bowl and whip attachment of your electric mixer are perfectly clean and grease-free. Beat the egg whites on low speed until frothy, then increase the speed to high and beat until soft peaks begin to form. Gradually sprinkle the sugar over the top, one tablespoon at a time, continuing to beat at high speed. When all the sugar is beaten in, add the vanilla, vinegar, and cornstarch. Beat until the egg whites are stiff but not dry, 2 or 3 minutes.

4. Spoon the meringue into a large pastry bag fitted with a large open star tip. Pipe a scalloped circle of meringue around the drawn circle on the parchment. Pipe another scalloped circle inside the first one. Then pipe a third circle on top of the seam of the first two, forming a tiered rim.

5. Bake the meringue in the preheated oven for 15 minutes. Reduce the heat to 205 degrees F [100 degrees C] and continue to bake for 1 hour. The meringue will be crisp on the outside and soft in the middle. Set aside on a wire rack to cool. Once the meringue is completely cool, you can store it in an airtight container.

To Prepare the Sauce

6. Warm the honey in a small saucepan over high heat. When it is thick and bubbly, add the nectarine skins and lemon zest. Cook, stirring constantly, for about 2 minutes to extract all the flavorful oils.

7. Stir in the cardamom and $1/4$ cup of the wine. Keep at a boil to reduce the wine, then add $1/4$ cup more wine. Reduce that, then add the remaining $1/2$ cup and simmer for 5 minutes. Strain the sauce, discarding the debris. Rinse the pan and pour in the strained liquid.

8. Mix the arrowroot with 4 teaspoons of water to make a slurry. Add the slurry to the sauce and stir over medium heat until it thickens and clears.

To Serve

9. Arrange the fruit artfully in the center of the meringue. Pour the sauce over the fruit to give it gloss. Slice into wedges and serve at the table.

Time Estimate

Hands-on, 45 minutes; unsupervised, 1 hour and 15 minutes.

Nutritional Profile per Serving

172 calories; 1 g fat; 0 g saturated fat; 3% of calories from fat; 39 g carbohydrate; 1 g dietary fiber.

Portability

Make the meringue shell at home and transport in an airtight container. The fruit can be prepared and transported in separate resealable bags and the sauce can be carried in a plastic container.

appetizer
Steamed Prawns and Oysters
Shellfish in a simple dish steaming with delicate traces of root ginger and chardonnay.

vegetarian option
Hearts of Palm and Mushrooms

main course
Swordfish Sydney
Bush tucker seasoning and fresh swordfish come dramatically encased in a parchment packet.

vegetarian option
Fennel Root Sydney

vegetable
Cauliflower and Carrots with Fennel Seeds
An attractive dish with plenty of color, flavor, and texture.

dessert
Potted Wattleseed Custard
Smooth custard infused with the elusive coffee and chocolate tastes of Australian wattleseed.

*S*ydney, Australia is a beautiful and exciting city, with one of the most dramatic entrances in the world. As we cruised smoothly into the harbor, the shadow of the Sydney Harbor Bridge fell across our decks, and across the water we could admire the modern Opera House with its lofty sail shapes, which locals refer to as a "clutch of nuns." We docked alongside the magnificent sandstone buildings of The Rocks, the oldest part of Sydney. It was a memorable entrance to a remarkable "gathering place."

According to archaeologists, humans have been gathering on this continent for thousands of years. There seems to be little doubt that Australia could well be the oldest continent in the world, with

SYDNEY
Foods of the Future

some of the oldest signs of civilization. Among its historic relics are millstones that have been judged to be over fifty thousand years

The variety of cuisines available in Sydney reflects its eclectic heritage.

old. If these prove to be accurately identified, it could mean that bread-making was an Australian invention. The Kerr family landed in Australia about 48,036 years after the earliest folks, having come from one of the newer continents up north. Even though Treena and I had lived in New Zealand for seven years prior to our arrival in Sydney in 1964, we were still regarded as transplanted Brits, or POMS [Prisoners of Mother England]. This is an affectionate [well, not always] term for the British who first colonized New South Wales [the east coast of Australia] in 1788 with surplus convicts from England's overcrowded jails.

Even though we were POMS, Treena and I spent a wonderful five years in this city, and if you take a tour of the inner harbor when you visit Sydney your guide may point out a tumbling white home with a large cedar boatshed. "That's where Graham Kerr [usually pronounced 'cur'] used to live...the Galloping Gourmet...that boatshed was his personal kitchen."

Previous page:
We film at the fish market in Sydney
These shellfish are called Balmain Bugs, Shovel Mouth Lobsters or Morton Bay Bugs!

This page, from top:
The Sydney Harbor Bridge and The Sydney Opera House ["a clutch of nuns"] welcome us "down under."

Vic Cherikoff, "entrepreneur of the outback."

Although Sydney had excellent restaurants and many fine chefs in those days, nothing could have prepared me for the explosion of creative cooking that has taken place over the past couple of decades, and Treena and I were keen to explore the city anew. Our visit was nonstop, starting with a trip to a botanical garden with Vic Cherikoff, also known as the entrepreneur of the outback. Vic is promoting the commercial use of some of the more than ten thousand indigenous foods of the Australian outback. His enthusiasm for Bush Tucker foods was contagious, and we sampled a number of these unique flavors over lunch at Edna's Table, a restaurant in the city center that is making the most of what Australia has to offer. Treena and I tasted kangaroo tail steaks in a delicious wild plum sauce and salmon baked in paperbark stripped from native melaleuca trees. We enjoyed a dessert made of native wattleseed, which tastes like a mixture of chocolate and coffee with hints of hazelnut and spice.

The variety of the cuisines available in Sydney reflects its eclectic heritage. There are almost four million people here from all over the world, and Sydney's food is the better for it. One international food critic, John Wells of England, has said, "The best food in Sydney is the best food in the world." My dear friend Ethel Hofman, former president of the International Association of Culinary Professionals, sees this city as an international trend-setter: "Sydney is a thrilling preview of what will most profoundly influence the cuisine of the 21st century." Sydney, more than any city I know, has truly made a shift to gourmet eating in a way that focuses on what is fresh, in season, and less dependent on excessive fats. It is, in my judgment, the world's most exciting food city.

As we sailed slowly out of the Sydney Harbor, the lights of this great city lit up the sky. The profiles of the Opera House and the bridge faded from sight, leaving a gleam in our eyes. We had tasted the future and wanted more! As we set off into the Tasman Sea, I thought about all the new combinations of flavors, textures, and aromas out there in the world, just waiting for folks like us who care about their health. Someone, somewhere in the Basque Mountains put onions, garlic, tomatoes, and basil together, so why not combine lemon myrtle and mountain pepper with seafood?

For our Sydney-style dinner, I have prepared a typical first course of lightly steamed rock oysters and large shrimp [Aussie prawns].

As we set off into the Tasman Sea, I thought about the flavors, textures, and aromas out there in the world, just waiting for folks like us who care about their health.

A six-ounce portion of swordfish inside a crackling parchment package makes a dramatic entrée, accompanied by fresh cauliflower and carrots. For dessert, you can shake your wattle bush and make a splendidly different wattleseed custard. All of this contains just 765 calories and 14 grams of fat for 16% of calories from fat. The vegetarian option features steamed fennel, baked in the same herbal mixture, with a total of 507 calories and only 7% of those from fat.

This page, from top:
Courtney Clark [*right*] makes sure we visit Sydney's Seafood School.

What good friends we've made on board!

As the QE II cruises out of the Sydney Harbor, Treena and I savor our memories.

Steamed Prawns and Oysters

You might say that the essential style of Sydney cuisine is a straightforward method of cooking that doesn't get in the way of great ingredients. This dish represents that attitude. Steaming keeps the seafood fresh and the ginger "drizzle" adds just the right amount of sparkle. Served on a bed of shredded cabbage, this appetizer is very attractive.

SERVES 6

Ginger Drizzle Sauce

   1/2 teaspoon light olive oil

    1 teaspoon fresh gingerroot, peeled and cut into fine matchsticks

   1/2 cup dry white wine [I prefer dealcoholized chardonnay]

Main Ingredients

    1 head savoy cabbage,* cut into 1/2-inch [1 1/2-cm] strips

   1/4 teaspoon salt

   1/4 teaspoon freshly ground black pepper

    1 teaspoon fresh gingerroot, peeled and cut into fine matchsticks

   18 medium prawns, peeled and deveined

   18 extra-small oysters,* on the half shell

Vegetarian Option [per Serving]

    1 heart of palm

    6 button mushrooms

    1 teaspoon fresh lemon juice

To Prepare the Sauce

1. Warm the oil in a small saucepan over medium-high heat. Sauté the ginger for 1 minute. Stir in the wine and set aside until ready to serve.

To Prepare the Shellfish and Cabbage

2. Scatter the cabbage on the bottom platform of a two-tiered steamer or place in a steamer insert. Sprinkle with the salt, pepper, and ginger. Cover and steam for 2 minutes.

---

*Savoy Cabbage

This light green, ruffled cabbage has a mild flavor and tender texture. Unlike red and green cabbage, it has a significant amount of beta carotene. If you've had trouble getting your family to eat cabbage, try savoy in coleslaws or other cabbage dishes. It takes about half as long to cook as its crispier cousins.

*Oysters

Oysters should be as fresh as possible—live is best. Ask your fishmonger to shuck them for you; unless you're an expert, it is probably worth whatever he charges you. Save the shells, wash them carefully, and use them for serving. They can be used again with very fresh oysters that are packed in jars. Choose extra small oysters if you plan to steam them.

3. Reduce the heat to low and lay the prawns over the top of the partially cooked cabbage. Place the oysters in the second platform and stack it on top. Cover and steam both levels for 2 minutes. If you do not have a two-tiered steamer, steam the prawns over the cabbage for 2 minutes, then transfer to covered bowls to keep warm while you steam the oysters.

To Serve

4. Spread a bed of cabbage on each salad plate, then arrange the oysters and prawns around a small bowl of "drizzle sauce" on each plate. Serve immediately.

Time Estimate

Hands-on, 25 minutes.

Nutritional Profile per Serving

175 calories; 4 g fat; 1 g saturated fat; 21% of calories from fat; 12 g carbohydrate; 2 g dietary fiber.

Vegetarian Option: Hearts and Palm and Mushrooms

Cut the heart of palm in half lengthwise and place in a steamer with the mushrooms. Cover and steam for 7 minutes. Season with the lemon juice and a light dusting of salt and pepper.

Vegetarian Option Nutritional Profile per Serving

70 calories; 1 g fat; 0 g saturated fat; 7% of calories from fat; 16 g carbohydrate; 3 g dietary fiber.

Portability

Carry the sliced cabbage in a resealable bag. Have the oysters and prawns ready to steam and the ginger cut. You may want to bring your own steamer. Everything here is last minute so prepare the dish at the party. The sizzling ginger will have everyone drooling.

Swordfish Sydney

In this lovely dish, swordfish seasoned with lemon myrtle and mountain pepper nestles on a bed of savory rice inside a crackling parchment package. There is enough unique "bush tucker" seasoning to qualify this dish with the name Sydney, but the flavors are quite subtle and do nothing to mask the taste of the fish. Paperbark would traditionally be used to wrap the fish, but parchment does a fine job of locking in the flavor and moistness of this dish. Serve Cauliflower and Carrots [page 207] as an accompaniment.

SERVES 6

Rice Pilaf

1/2	teaspoon light olive oil
1	cup finely diced onion
1 1/2	cups long-grain white rice
1/2	teaspoon salt
1/4	teaspoon white pepper
3	cups low-sodium chicken or vegetable stock

Fish

1	teaspoon light olive oil
1	tablespoon fresh lemon juice
1/2	teaspoon powdered lemon myrtle* or dried lemon thyme
1/4	teaspoon salt
1/2	teaspoon white pepper
1/2	teaspoon mountain pepper,* optional
2 1/4	pounds [1 kg] swordfish,* cut into 6 slices
1	teaspoon paprika
6	fresh bay leaves

Vegetarian Option [per Serving]

2	small fennel roots [about 6 ounces or 170 g], trimmed

1. Preheat the oven to 450 degrees F [230 degrees C].

To Prepare the Rice Pilaf

2. Warm the oil in a medium saucepan over medium-high heat.

---

*Swordfish

This large saltwater fish is a highly prized game and commercial fish. It has a very firm light-colored meat with a distinctive but delicate flavor. You could substitute fresh tuna or Chilean sea bass.

*Australian Flavorings

This dinner party makes use of a number of tastes unique to Australia. I feel sure that these herbs and seeds will become staple items in the global cuisine of the future but, for the time being, they may seem quite exotic.

* Lemon myrtle comes from a rainforest tree that grows on the east coast of Australia. It has a complex flavor that seems to combine lemongrass, lemon and lime oil flavors and is a perfect complement to fish. It can be used fresh or dried.

* Mountain pepper comes from a leaf which can be used whole or ground. It has a mellow, peppery flavor with just a bit of heat. You can substitute black pepper and bay.

Australian ingredients can be ordered from:

Bush Tucker Supply Australia
P.O. Box B 103
Boronia Park N.S.W. 2111 Australia

Phone: 011-61-2-817-1060
Fax: 011-61-2-817-3587.

Sauté the onion for 3 minutes, or until soft but not browned.

3. Stir in the rice, salt, and pepper. Cook for an additional 2 minutes, stirring often. Add the stock. [Vegetarian Option: Use vegetable stock.] Cover, bring to a boil, then reduce the heat and simmer for 15 minutes.

To Prepare the Fish

4. You will need 6 pieces of baking parchment measuring 12 inches x 16 inches [30 cm x 41 cm]. Stack the pieces in a neat pile and fold them in half, short end to short end, so that you have an 8 x 12-inch [20 x 30-cm] rectangle. Using the folded edge as the center, draw a half-heart shape on the parchment, making the dimensions as large as possible. [After the paper is cut and unfolded, a whole heart will emerge]. Cut along the outline through all the layers.

5. Combine the oil and lemon juice and brush on a cookie sheet. Sprinkle the lemon myrtle, salt, white pepper, and optional mountain pepper evenly over the oiled pan.

6. Lay the fish fillets on top of the seasonings, then turn them over, so that the rub adheres to both sides of the fish. [Vegetarian Option: Roll the steamed fennel roots in the seasonings before you coat the fish.]

7. Unfold one of the parchment hearts and lay flat. Spoon $^1/_3$ cup of the cooked rice onto the right-hand side of the heart. Lay the seasoned fish on top of the rice. Sprinkle the fillet with paprika and top with a bay leaf. Fold the left half of the heart over the fish and align the edges of the parchment. Starting with a small section at the top of the heart, fold the edges together, crease, and fold again, as if making a narrow hem. Work your way around the curve of the heart a small section at a time. Each new section will overlap the end of the previous section, like a series of pleats. When you have finished the folds, give the rim a good pinch to seal the package thoroughly. Repeat with the remaining packages.

8. Place on a baking sheet lightly coated with cooking spray. Store

in the refrigerator until ready to cook. Spray the tops of the packages lightly before baking.

9. Bake in the preheated oven for 8 to 12 minutes, depending on whether the packages have been chilled. Open one of the packets to check for doneness—the fish should be just barely cooked through, since it will continue cooking as you prepare the plates for serving.

To Serve

10. Place a package in the center of a warmed dinner plate. Cut a large X across the top of the paper with scissors and roll back the parchment to reveal the ingredients. Serve Cauliflower with Carrots on the side.

Time Estimate

Hands-on, 40 minutes; unsupervised, 23 minutes.

Nutritional Profile per Serving

413 calories; 8 g fat; 2 g saturated fat; 18% of calories from fat; 41 g carbohydrate; 1 g dietary fiber.

Vegetarian Option

Cut the fennel roots in half lengthwise and steam for 5 minutes. Cool and proceed exactly as you would with the fish.

Vegetarian Option Nutritional Profile per Serving

260 calories; 1 g fat; 0 g saturated fat; 5% of calories from fat; 53 g carbohydrate; 1 g dietary fiber.

Cauliflower and Carrots with Fennel Seeds

This is a very attractive vegetable dish with great color, flavor, and texture.

Serves 6

- 2 heads cauliflower, broken or cut into flowerettes [6 cups]
- 1 teaspoon fennel seeds
- 1/4 teaspoon salt
- 6 medium carrots, peeled and cut on the diagonal into 1/4-inch [3/4-cm] slices [2 cups]

1. Place the cauliflower flowerettes on the bottom platform of a two-tiered steamer. Sprinkle the fennel seeds and salt over the top. Place the carrots in the second platform and stack it on top. Place both over the boiling water, cover, and steam 8 minutes for crisp-tender vegetables or 12 minutes if you like them softer. If you do not have a two-tiered steamer, steam the vegetables in two batches, keeping the cauliflower warm while the carrots cook.

2. Combine the cauliflower and carrots and serve.

Time Estimate
Hands-on, 15 minutes; unsupervised, 8 or 12 minutes.

Nutritional Profile per Serving
66 calories; 1 g fat; 0 g saturated fat; 9% of calories from fat; 14 g carbohydrate; 6 g dietary fiber.

Potted Wattleseed Custard

Wattleseed is an extraordinary taste sensation, a mix of hazelnut and coffee and chocolate notes. Besides being an authentic taste of Australia, it is a delicious way to end a great meal. This smooth potted custard recipe can be used with dozens of different flavors that rely upon natural concentrated essences—experiment!

SERVES 6

$1^{1}/_{2}$ cups evaporated skim milk
$1^{1}/_{2}$ cups 2% milk
$^{1}/_{4}$ cup brown sugar
2 tablespoons wattleseeds* or 2 tablespoons Postum™ and 1 tablespoon instant coffee
$^{1}/_{2}$ teaspoon vanilla extract
1 cup egg substitute [I prefer Egg Beaters™]

1. Preheat the oven to 325 degrees F [165 degrees C].

To Prepare the Custard Using Wattleseeds

2. Combine the two kinds of milk, brown sugar, and wattleseeds in a large saucepan.

3. Cook the mixture over medium heat just to the point of boiling. Remove from the heat and set aside for 10 or 15 minutes to allow the milk to absorb as much flavor as possible.

4. Strain through a cheesecloth into another saucepan and stir in the vanilla and egg substitute.

5. Pour the custard into six 6-ounce [177-ml] custard cups. Arrange the cups in a baking dish and set in the oven. Pull the rack out slightly and pour enough hot water into the baking dish to come about 3/4 of the way up the sides of the cups.

6. Bake for 50 to 60 minutes, or until a knife inserted in the center of each custard comes out perfectly clean. As soon as they are cool enough to handle, take the cups out of the water bath and allow to cool on a rack.

To Prepare the Custard Using Postum™

1. Combine the two kinds of milk in a large saucepan and heat until almost boiling.

2. Add the Postum™ and instant coffee, stirring to dissolve. Add the brown sugar, stirring until it is completely dissolved. Stir in the vanilla and egg substitute.

3. Proceed with Step 5 of Method 1.

To Serve

7. The custards can be served at room temperature or chilled. Attractive 6-ounce [177-ml] containers, like small French soufflé dishes or custard cups, help a great deal with the presentation.

Time Estimate

Hands-on, 20 minutes; unsupervised, 1 hour.

Nutritional Profile per Serving

111 calories; 1 g fat; 1 g saturated fat; 10% of calories from fat; 14 g carbohydrate; 0 g dietary fiber.

Portability

This dessert can be made a day or so ahead and carried to the party in the baking dishes.

Bash 'n Chop

Citrus Juicer

Fat Strainer

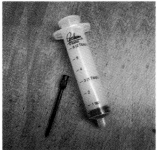

Flavor Injector

During the past few decades that I have spent cooking for others, I've grown to believe that a great deal of pleasure can come from simple tasks performed well. This chapter is meant to give you more information about tools, techniques and ingredients that have been mentioned elsewhere in "The Gathering Place." These resources can help you achieve successful change in the way you eat and prepare food for your family and friends. I have collected a number of my favorites here. Some of them are very simple, everyday sorts of things. Others are special tools or techniques I've developed or adapted that can help you save time in the kitchen or reduce the amount of excessive, harmful fats or sugars in your cooking. I hope they'll provide a springboard for you to use in developing your own creative, inventive way to cook for those you love.

Tools

Bash 'n Chop
One of my earliest signature pieces, this broad knife helps you bash, crush, core, scoop, and measure.

Citrus Juicer
Heart-healthy recipes really wake up and come to attention with the addition of fresh lemon or orange juice. This device juices, separates seeds from the juice, and stores the unused portion. Perfect!

Fat Strainer
This is an indispensable tool for anyone who wants to eliminate excess fat from their food. Shaped like a measuring cup with a long spout, it is very easy to use. Pour hot liquid into the cup, wait for the fat to rise to the top, then pour out the defatted liquid from the bottom.

Flavor Injector
This device adds flavor to meat, fruits, and vegetables—from the inside out! It's easy to use, and you'll soon be concocting your own creative marinades.

Meat Thermometer
Bayonet-type meat thermometers read temperatures instantly; they are quite accurate and inexpensive. Even the cheap ones can be reset

by plunging the thermometer into boiling water [212 degrees F or 100 degrees C] and adjusting a knob at the base of the thermometer head. Digital thermometers are easier to read.

MEV

Melon Baller

This old-fashioned tool hasn't changed much over the years. I like the ones with a different size scoop on each end of a plastic or wooden handle.

MEV

Like a large muffin tin with a detachable lid, the MEV tray is used to bake layers of interesting, flavorful ingredients. The completed molds add height, drama, and interest to the dinner plate. Complete directions and recipes are included.

Olive Oil Pump

Olive Oil Pump

Even healthful olive oil, when used in excess, can add far too many calories to your day. I've reduced the oil I need for a simple sauté to a skimpy $1/2$ teaspoon, measured for you by this stainless steel pump dispenser.

Purée Press

Many fruits and vegetables have skins or fibers that should be removed in order to produce a smoother presentation. I use a mushroom-shaped tool I designed specifically for this purpose; it greatly speeds up the task of sieving food.

Salad Dressing Shaker

Salad Spinner

Dressing adheres best to dry salad greens, and this device is handy for spinning them. I often add a small amount of dressing, too—the spinner distributes it more evenly than I can do by hand and the greens pick up lots of flavor from very little dressing.

Salad Dressing Shaker

Why not make fresh salad dressing? You'll add flavor and aroma to the most humble of greens. Five of my favorite recipes are printed on the bottle, along with measurements.

Slimmer Skimmer

Slimmer Skimmer

Fats and oils run into the slots along the rim of this stainless steel ladle and collect in the bottom. The other side can be used as a regular ladle.

Tools, Techniques and Ingredients

Slurry Cup

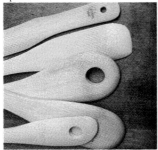

Spurtles

Yogurt Strainer

° Slurry Cup

A key to many of my healthy techniques is the use of cornstarch or arrowroot to thicken sauces instead of fats, flour, and butter . This little device helps spin the thickener with a liquid to make a smooth slurry and can double as a vinaigrette shaker, too.

Steamer

This is a key piece of equipment for anyone learning to cook with less fat and more flavor. There are many different brands of steamer, but I use a "stack and steam" arrangement where two steaming racks can be fitted over a saucepan. Choose a stacking steamer that will accommodate an 8-inch [20-cm] dinner plate [that means a 10-inch [25-cm] diameter steamer base].

° Spurtles

I love these flat bamboo cooking utensils. They're specially shaped to reach into the corners of pots and pans, bringing up every bit of tasty goodness.

Vertical Roaster

This is a very sensible gadget that allows a chicken to roast upright in the oven. Hot oven air can circulate evenly around the bird, and the fat drains into a baking pan placed underneath [a cup of water will prevent spattering], producing juicy and flavorful results. I prefer a clay roaster and often stuff the cavity of the chicken with fresh herbs.

° Yogurt Strainer

Substituting strained yogurt for butter or other high-fat spreads could reduce your fat consumption by 47,000 calories per year. Toss a carton of yogurt into the strainer set over a bowl and place in the refrigerator. Next day, you'll have a thick, creamy mixture that's ready to spread on toast or use in sauces. Use a plain, nonfat yogurt without gelatin.

Techniques

Browned Onion Sauces
Slowly caramelize onions over low heat and use as the base for a rich, dark sauce for a number of hearty dishes.

Cooking Spray
I used to turn up my nose at aerosol cooking sprays until I began to experiment with them. Used properly, they can dramatically reduce the amount of oil you need for cooking. Try spritzing the top of meats and vegetables that are headed for the broiler to achieve an appetizing sheen with virtually no added fat.

Corn [cutting]
First, trim the stalk end of an ear of corn to make a flat base so that the cob will hold steady. Slice from the top to the bottom, holding a sharp knife parallel to the cob. You don't want to cut too deep or not deep enough—too deep and you will cut off woody pieces of the cob, not deep enough and you will miss out on the sweet white juices of the kernels.

Etoufée
A French word that means "smothered," this classic technique is used to express volatile oils and steam food in a covered pan. Food is browned, then surrounded by aromatic ingredients and simmered in a small amount of flavorful liquid. Used with fresh herbs and vegetables, this method can produce an explosion of satisfying fragrance and aroma with the use of very little fat.

Fruit Purées
Substitute fruit purées for part of the fat in cakes, cookies, muffins, and other baked goods.

Handling Hot Chile Peppers
The membranes and seeds of hot chiles contain capsaicin, the chemical compound that gives chile peppers their heat and can irritate skin. Wear rubber gloves while you're working with hot peppers or scrub your hands with soap and water afterward. If you only need 2 or 3 tablespoons of minced chile for a recipe, cut out a portion of one side, leaving the rest of the pepper intact. You'll find the chile stays fresher while stored in a plastic bag in the refrigerator, and you'll handle fewer seeds.

Maillard Reaction
As tomato paste cooks in a nonstick pan, the natural sugars

Throughout the research and preparation of this book, I have held to one absolute maxim: "Cooking is an act of kindness when it is caring wrapped in pleasure."

This assumes that the food you prepare is chosen with health in mind. Good health isn't simply a matter of lower fat choices and more fresh vegetables. It's also a matter of being aware of the harm that can result from the mishandling of food.

Because this book involves groups of people gathering together, there is likely to be some distance involved in preparing and carrying the food from one kitchen to another. I thought it would make good sense to review a few ways to keep food safe.

In 1997, I served as the chairman of the National Food Safety Education Month sponsored by the Industry Council on Food Safety. It was an enlightening experience, and I grew to appreciate the value of this often overlooked issue. Here are my "top ten" tips, based on decades of experience as well as my recent tenure as chairman:

1. Illness, infections, or stomach upsets can put others at risk; best not to handle or prepare food for others at those times.

2. Always begin by giving your hands a good scrub with an antibacterial soap and plenty of warm water. Wash again after handling raw meat or poultry. Use paper towels for drying your hands.

caramelize. This is a handy way to deepen and enrich the flavor of sauces and stews.

Meat in the Minor Key
Supplement smaller portions of meat with imaginatively presented vegetables and whole grains for a satisfying meal.

Peeled, Bashed, and Chopped
This is my favorite way to deal with garlic cloves and a number of other ingredients. You'll find my Bash 'n Chop to be very useful, but a chef's knife will also work.

Pineapple [cutting]
To prepare a pineapple shell for filling, use a long, narrow knife and make a flat cut across the top of the pineapple to remove the leaves and a portion of the top. Leave the bottom intact. Slip the knife inside the rind and cut around the inside of the shell, just deep enough to separate the flesh from the shell. Go around the perimeter a couple of times to be sure the flesh is completely loosened from the rind. Turn the pineapple on its side. Insert the knife into the base and work it around inside each side. Remove the pineapple flesh, pulling the rind off in one piece. Cut the flesh lengthwise into 4 wedges and remove the coarse core. Rinse out the shell and freeze until firm. Set the shell upright in a cake pan and fill with a frozen dessert for a dramatic presentation.

Poultry Skin
Sauté, broil, grill, or roast poultry with its skin intact, then remove and discard the skin before serving. The meat will stay moist, but as low in fat as if it were cooked without the skin.

Reductions
Increase the flavor of poultry, vegetable, or wine-based stocks by boiling them until they are reduced in volume.

Rice and Cheese Crusts
Use rice, Parmesan cheese, seasonings, and an egg white to make low-fat crusts for quiches and savory pies.

Roasted Meat Gravies
Strain the fat from cooking juices and add dealcoholized wine [I prefer Ariel] or fruit juice to make flavorful low-fat gravies.

Roasted Vegetables

Familiar vegetables can be transformed into smoky, sweet sensations by roasting them in a very hot oven.

Serving Plates

More than fifty percent of Americans are now considered obese; I believe that the huge portions we are accustomed to eating may have something to do with that. Smaller, more reasonable-sized portions often look more dramatic when served on a plate with a wide rim and smaller serving area. Do take a moment to warm plates before serving; a few moments in the microwave or a warm oven will provide a special caring touch.

Slurry

Mix a small amount of arrowroot or cornstarch with liquid [water, stock, fruit juice, or dealcoholized wine] to make a slurry. These slurries will quickly thicken sauces and soups and will add a gloss to many sauces that is often missing in low-fat cooking. I often use arrowroot because it thickens without boiling, but please experiment. Too much and it turns to jelly.

Smooth Vegetable Sauces

Use cooked, puréed vegetables that have been seasoned with herbs and spices as a flavor-filled base for sauces, vegetables, and casseroles.

Thickening with Starch

Use pure starches [such as arrowroot or cornstarch] to thicken sauces and gravies. They require no added fat to "glisten."

Vinaigrette and Broth for Sauces

Replace a portion of the oil in vinaigrettes with broths or juices to make tasty, low-fat sauces and dressings.

White Sauces

Make rich coating sauces with yogurt cheese, cornstarch, and cooking liquids instead of using fat-based sauces.

Yogurt Cheese

See "Yogurt Strainer" in section above.

3. Clean cutting boards and knives thoroughly after preparing raw meat, poultry, or seafood. Use an antibacterial disinfectant to wipe counters and other surfaces.

4. Never taste food with your fingers or the same spoon you use to stir.

5. Harmful bacteria multiply quickly when given ideal conditions of warmth and moisture. Most vulnerable are soups, stocks, sauces, meats, chicken, and milk products. Keep cold foods cold [40 degrees or below] and hot foods above 140 degrees until serving.

6. Wash fresh produce in a sink used only for this rinsing. Harmful bacteria can be present in soil and should be kept off working surfaces.

7. Make the grocery store the last stop when shopping and running errands. Get all perishable items back into the refrigerator within two hours of purchase.

8. Avoid defrosting frozen meat, poultry, or seafood at room temperature. The refrigerator is safer. Once defrosted, avoid refreezing.

9. Cover everything with a tight-fitting lid. Store sealed cooked food above raw food and never let the two touch.

10. When transporting cooked food, keep it as cool as possible and well protected.

Ingredients

Angostura Bitters
   Used in small amounts, angostura bitters lend an aromatic and slightly bitter element to mixed drinks. Made in Trinidad from roots, bark, leaves, and alcohol, these bitters can be found in the beverage department of your supermarket.

Australian Flavors
   Lemon myrtle comes from a rainforest tree that grows on the east coast of Australia. It has a complex flavor that seems to combine lemongrass, lemon and lime oil flavors and is a perfect complement to fish. It can be used fresh or dried.

   Mountain pepper comes from a leaf that can be used whole or ground. It has a mellow, peppery flavor with just a bit of heat. You can substitute black pepper and bay.

   Wattles are shrubs or small trees of the acacia family. There are over 900 different wattle varieties in Australia, but only 100 or so are used for food. The fruits of these plants are long beans, the seeds of which are roasted and ground to make beverages and flavorings. Wattleseed tastes like a combination of coffee, chocolate, and hazelnuts.

   To order Australian ingredients, contact:
   Bush Tucker Supply Australia
   P. O. Box B 103
   Boronia Park N.S.W. 2111

   Phone: 61 [02] 9817-1060
   Fax: 61 [02] 9817-3587

Bean Flours
   When beans are ground to a fine flour, they cook very quickly. None of the nutritional value or flavor is lost in the grinding. Bean flours make wonderful instant soup and sauce bases. Chickpea [garbanzo bean] flour can be made into instant hummus with the addition of lemon, garlic, and a little tahini. Look for bean flours in supermarkets, natural food stores, or contact:

   Bob's Red Mill Natural Foods, Inc.
   5209 S.E. International Way
   Milwaukie, Oregon 97222

   Phone: [503] 654-3215
   Fax: [503] 653-1339

Belgian Endive

This handsome member of the chicory family is slightly bitter and arrives in a small, tightly packed head, like tiny romaine. It is grown in the dark, so it is pale yellow or white and is wonderful mixed with mild greens or used as a packet for appetizers.

Bok Choy

I love this Asian member of the cabbage family. Its thick white stem is crunchy, and its leaves are the tiniest bit bitter—a great combination in a single vegetable.

Canadian Bacon

Lower in fat than regular bacon, this is a useful ingredient for adding a smoky, salty flavor many people enjoy. Very little is needed to add the bright notes of flavor many dishes require.

Cake Flour

Milled from soft wheat, cake flour has less gluten than other flours, so it helps keep low-fat baked goods more tender.

Celeriac

Pronounced "seh-LER-ee-ak," this brown, knobby root mass has a wonderful flavor that is a combination of celery and parsley. It is delicious in puréed soups and marinated salads. Also called celery root, it's available from fall until spring, handy for those of us searching for fresh and best in winter! Choose smooth, firm roots that weigh less than a pound. If wrapped in plastic and refrigerated, they should keep a week or more. Remove the stalk and scrub the root with a brush. Cut off any protruding knobs and peel with a vegetable peeler or paring knife.

Chicken Stock

Canned chicken stock has an alarming amount of sodium, so I urge you to search out a low-sodium variety. The taste can be boosted considerably by simmering it with a few sprigs of parsley or your favorite herbs and a bit of lemongrass. If you prefer to make your own, it freezes beautifully in resealable plastic bags.

Chiles

A number of recipes in this book call for roasted chile peppers. You could certainly buy fresh Anaheim chiles and roast them, but there are so many great ways to use chiles that I recommend buying diced green chiles in a can. About a pound of fresh chiles will produce an ounce of roasted, peeled chiles.

Cocoa

I use cocoa in place of other forms of chocolate in baking to achieve a rich flavor without the fat. I usually choose Dutch or European-style cocoa because they are less acid and have a rich, mellow flavor.

Coconut Essence and Desiccated Coconut

I prefer coconut extracts or essences made from natural sources, because artificial coconut flavorings have a strong chemical smell that gives an "off" taste to an entire dish. John Wagner and Sons makes an excellent natural coconut essence that can be found in any well-stocked grocery or gourmet food store. For information, call [800] 832-9017.

Desiccated coconut is simply coconut that has been dried, thus concentrating its flavor. It can be found in specialty and natural food stores.

Couscous

These little bits of semolina dough coated with wheat flour are a staple food in a number of countries, particularly North Africa. Large-grain couscous has grains about the size of peppercorns, while regular couscous is very similar to Cream of Wheat in size. I use Middle Eastern-style couscous from Pitter's Pantry. If you're unable to find it, call the Specialty Foods Manager at Larry's Markets in Bellevue, Washington, at [206] 453-0600.

Dealcoholized Wine

I like to use dealcoholized wine in my recipes and prefer Ariel because the folks there produce classic, finely crafted wines that have had the alcohol removed by a cold centrifuge process.

Dried Fruits

Dried fruits are intensely flavored and provide textural interest to many dishes. Look beyond dried apricots and raisins to dried cranberries, strawberries, blueberries, and cherries. Natural food stores often have a nice selection. For direct mail sales, contact: Chukar Cherry Company, Inc. at [800] 624-9544.

Duck Breasts

To remove breasts from a whole duck, use a sharp knife to sever the drumsticks. With the duck breast-down on the cutting surface, remove the wings, preserving as much breast meat as possible. Turn the duck over and cut just through the skin and down the center between the two breasts. Gently cut meat away from the breast

bones and the ribs, using the tip of the knife and lifting the meat away from the bones with your fingers. If you are interested in obtaining boneless, frozen duck breasts call:
D'Artagna, Inc. at [800] 327-8246.

Egg Substitutes

These are eggs with the yolks removed and can be used in many egg dishes as well as for baking. After many taste tests, we found we prefer Egg Beaters™.

Garam Masala

Garam masala is an Indian spice mixture usually added at the end of cooking. It is composed of cinnamon, cardamom, cloves, cumin, and other "warming" spices. If you can't find a good variety at your market, try this combination:

1   thin cinnamon stick, about 2 inches [10 cm] long
6   allspice berries
$1/4$ teaspoon nutmeg
4   whole cloves

Blend to a powder in a small electric coffee grinder designated for this purpose. Shake through a sieve and store in a small jar.

Green-Lipped Mussels

These mussels are grown in New Zealand and have a beautiful green stripe around their shells. They are large, sweet, and always available frozen, if you will ask your fishmonger to order them. You can certainly substitute our more common blue mussels, but you'll need two to three times as many.

Habañero Chile

The habañero is the hottest of all chiles—1,000 times hotter than a jalapeño! It is bright yellow-orange, shaped like a lantern, and should be handled only while wearing plastic gloves. It is used fresh throughout South America, Brazil, the Caribbean, and the Yucatan Peninsula. Similar to Scotch Bonnets, habañeros may be found in your supermarket or a good Latin American grocery.

Hatcho Miso

Miso is a fermented soybean product that is essential to Japanese cooking. Low in calories and a good source of amino acids, vitamins, and minerals, miso enhances the flavor of soups, sauces, and other dishes. Hatcho miso is a special miso that has been made by the Hatcho Miso Company in Okazaki, Japan, for five centuries. It is made in the traditional way with whole soybeans and a small amount of water and has 80% more protein and 25% less salt than rice and barley misos. Look for labels such as Mitoku Macrobiotic, Erewhon, Westbrae, and Tree of Life at your supermarket or a good natural foods store.

Hearts of Palm

These are the tender inside layers of the palmetto palm, which grows in Florida and South America. The thick white cylinders will remind you of artichoke hearts and can serve as a low-fat option in a number of salads and other dishes. You'll find them canned in jars at any good supermarket.

Hominy

Hominy is made from dried corn kernels from which the hull and germ have been removed, usually by boiling in lime. The kernels look somewhat like popcorn and have a soft, chewy consistency. Hominy is sold either in canned or dried form. The canned version has a very high salt content, so you may want to try to find it dry. One mail order source is:

Indian Harvest Specialty Foods, Inc.
P.O. Box 428
Bemidji, MN 56619-0428

[800] 294-2433.

Kabocha Squash

This small, round Japanese pumpkin has dark green skin and grayish stripes and usually weights 2 or 3 pounds. The flesh is thick, yellow-orange, and very fine in texture, which makes these squash perfect for stuffing. Like other winter squash, they are available in fall and winter.

Lamb Shanks

Shanks from lambs raised in the United States tend to be quite large. Ask your butcher for small New Zealand or Australian lamb shanks, which provide a more moderate serving size.

Lemongrass

A versatile herb that adds a subtle fruity perfume to a variety of foods, lemongrass is becoming more available in American supermarkets. It is sold in long stalks with a bulb on one end. Peel the dry outer layers and cut the bulb into thin slices for dishes in which it will be eaten. Cut the outer stalk into 2-inch pieces and use to flavor stocks and sauces; remove the pieces before serving. Dried lemongrass is used for herbal teas, but I do not recommend it for flavoring food.

Lychee

This fruit is native to China and is now grown in tropical climates of the United States. It is available fresh in Asian markets during the summer months and canned year-round. The fruit is covered with a thin, brittle, slightly bumpy shell that is easily removed with your fingers. The fruit inside is white, soft, and somewhat like a grape. It has a marvelous aroma that is not lost during the canning process.

Mammee

Native to the West Indies and northern South America, this fruit is about the size of a large orange and has pale beige skin. Its soft, salmon-pink to dark red flesh is somehow reminiscent of a plum or an apricot. If you are unable to find it, you may order it during summer months from:

Robert Is Here
19900 S.W. 344th Street
Homestead, FL 33034-1408

[305] 246-1592

Mangoes

To choose a mango, look for one that gives slightly to soft pressure from the palm of your hand. California "Keitt" mangoes are ripe when their skin is dark green and the flesh is soft; the more common mangoes have orange skins. Mangoes have a long flat pit that lays horizontally through the middle of the fruit and can be difficult to remove. The best method I have found is to lay the palm of your hand over the mango, steadying the fruit horizontally against the table. To loosen the fruit from the pit, angle the knife blade up over the top of the pit, using a sawing motion and just touching the pit itself with the knife blade. When one side is loosened, turn the mango over and make another cut, using the same sawing motion. This will leave you with two halves and a pit. Trim any remaining flesh from the pit. Cut each half into four wedges and peel each wedge, running a thin knife blade between the flesh and the peel.

Masa Harina

This flour, made from dried hominy, is a staple in Mexican cuisine, where it is used to make bread, tortillas, tamales, and other foods. Masa dough may be found fresh in Mexican groceries, if you are lucky enough to have one in your community, but the flour is widely available in any supermarket.

Orange Roughy

This small saltwater fish is imported from New Zealand and only recently began appearing in my supermarket, usually in frozen form. The fillets are pure white with a delicate flavor.

Passion Fruit

This small, round, dark purple fruit is native to Brazil but can be found seasonally in markets throughout the world. A ripe one should have deeply wrinkled, yellowish-orange skin with a very soft interior. Choose the largest, heaviest fruit. The seeds are edible, but if you prefer to remove them, press the pulp through a sieve or twist through a cheesecloth.

Pohole

Pronounced "po-HOH-lay," this fern grows in tropical rain forests, with fronds ranging from three to six feet long. The young, tender fronds can be eaten raw in salads. This is a special treat for your guests that is worth pursuing. To order, try:

René and Eileen Comeaux
Hana Herbs
P.O. Box 323
Hana, Maui, Hawaii 96713

Phone or fax: [808] 248-7407

Pomegranate

This fruit is an important player in the flavors of Eastern and Mediterranean cuisines. It turns up in our supermarkets in fall and early winter and keeps well if refrigerated. The tart seeds provide a wonderful brightness and interesting texture to many dishes. Paula Wolfort, a notable expert on Middle Eastern and Mediterranean cuisines, suggests separating the seeds from the pulp in a bowl of water; the seeds sink and the pulp floats.

Rice Vinegar

You'll have no trouble finding this in your local supermarket. Made in China and Japan, it is more mellow than distilled vinegar. Cider vinegar is an acceptable substitute.

Saffron

The dried powder from the stigmas of a certain crocus that grows in the Middle East, this rare and expensive spice has a wonderful penetrating flavor and a glorious buttery color. Saffron is available in two forms: threads and powder. Powdered saffron is quite useful for finely textured sauces, but it is important to buy from a reputable vendor so you know that you are getting the real thing. Saffron threads may be less expensive and can be used anywhere that the tiny threads will not detract from the texture of the dish.

Savoiardi

These crisp Italian ladyfingers are low in fat, mild in flavor, and keep their shape. This makes them ideal for low-fat desserts as well as by themselves with tea or coffee. Look for the Ferrara brand in a specialty food store or contact:

Calavati
2537 Brunswick Avenue
Lynden, NY 07036

[908] 651-7600

Savoy Cabbage

This light green, ruffled cabbage has a mild flavor, tender texture, and a significant amount of beta carotene. Your family may prefer it in coleslaws or other cabbage dishes. It cooks faster than regular cabbage, too.

Sea Bass

Moist, tender, and white, this fish has a wonderful "mouthfeel" but very little fat. People who are reducing the amount of red meat in their diets often find sea bass very satisfying. Also called Patagonian Tooth Fish, these sea monsters weigh in at thirty to sixty pounds and live in the deep subtropical waters of South America and Africa. Sea bass freezes very well, and you can almost always find it frozen in your supermarket.

Serrano Chiles.

These small dark green or red peppers look like small jalapeños and are second only to habañeros in heat. If you include the seeds from the chiles, the dish will be very hot; without seeds, it will be somewhat milder. Available fresh or canned.

Soy Milk

I use soy milk in soups and creamy dessert sauces because it seems to make them smoother and more velvety. The health benefit of soy products is a special bonus.

Spice Mixes

You may be able to find ethnic blends of spices in your local gourmet store. I have found them an excellent way to add depth and flavor to everyday dishes, and I hope they will soon be available everywhere. In the meantime, a few moments spent blending a mix in a clean coffee grinder will give you a reserve to use for weeks to come.

Summer Savory

This versatile herb is a wonderful companion to beans and perks up soups beautifully. You may find it fresh in markets or produce sections—it's an easy herb to grow from seed, too.

Swordfish

This large saltwater fish is a highly prized game and commercial fish with a firm, light-colored meat and a distinctive but delicate flavor. You could substitute fresh tuna or Chilean sea bass.

Tamari

This high-quality Japanese soy sauce derives its rich flavor from amino acids and soy protein. It is made from fermenting soybeans with little or no wheat and is stronger in flavor and darker in color than other Japanese soy sauces. It contains no alcohol, so it can be simmered without its flavor evaporating. Look for low-sodium versions, which you may find in your supermarket, an Asian market, or a natural food store.

Taro Root

This tuber probably originated in East India, although it is grown in the Pacific Islands, Asia, the Caribbean, North Africa, and parts of Central and South America. Its texture is somewhere between potatoes and chestnuts. After peeling, it can be steamed and lightly mashed or stir-fried. I order taro root from my local produce manager, but you may also find it in Asian markets. You may want to wear gloves when you peel the roots as they may irritate your skin.

Thai Fish Sauce

Nam pla is as essential to Thai cooking as soy sauce is to Chinese.

It is a clear, salty liquid made from salted fermented fish. It is used as an ingredient in many dishes and in dipping sauces. It has a powerful smell but a mellow flavor that seems to enhance other flavors in a dish. It is rich in Vitamin B and will keep indefinitely with very little loss of color or flavor. It can be found in many supermarkets and most Asian groceries.

Tofu

After experimenting with this versatile product, I have found that I prefer Mori-Nu Lite Silken Tofu. It is low in fat and calories and doesn't need to be refrigerated. You will find it in natural food stores or good supermarkets. I like the extra-firm variety in most recipes.

Tuna

Yellowfin, called *Ahi* in Hawaii, plays a major part in the California tuna industry. It is eaten raw as sashimi or served quite rare in California cuisine. When cooked, it is darker than albacore and lighter than bluefin. It is usually available, fresh or frozen, in supermarket fish departments throughout the U.S. If you don't see it, ask your fishmonger to order it for you.

Unsulfured Molasses

Light molasses comes from the first boiling of the juices, dark molasses from the second, and blackstrap molasses from the last. Sulfur dioxide is sometimes used to lighten the syrup, but it leaves an unpleasant aftertaste. I recommend unsulfured molasses; if the label says unsulfured, or nothing at all, no sulfur has been used.

Yellow Finn Potatoes

Yellow Finns, grown in bumper crops in the Skagit Valley near my home, are small, oval, often irregular potatoes with a yellow skin and meat. Boasting a rich buttery flavor, they are excellent for boiling, baking, and roasting.

Nutritional Summary

fat	saturated fat	protein	carbohy.	sodium	calcium	iron	vitamin A	vitamin C	fiber	% from fat
0	0	1	10	8	5	0	46	12	1	4%
5	1	17	57	503	172	5	101	22	13	13%
1	0	2	9	65	9	1	114	35	2	14%
3	1	8	34	82	188	1	66	62	3	14%
4	1	5	20	221	71	1	167	70	2	26%
4	1	32	8	217	31	1	444	22	1	16%
0	0	2	10	161	13	1	357	17	0	3%
2	1	6	2	80	19	0	6	19	2	12%
1	0	6	9	56	49	1	167	57	4	14%
0	0	5	44	147	20	2	4	9	3	1%
2	0	11	6	356	156	4	777	37	4	21%
7	2	29	40	223	158	4	2511	195	7	19%
3	0	20	75	198	300	7	3474	254	19	7%
2	1	8	41	109	229	1	86	6	1	8%
7	2	10	22	438	90	2	169	31	4	34%
10	4	28	18	331	56	3	52	93	4	32%
4	0	5	23	264	56	2	53	103	4	23%
1	0	5	34	148	34	2	3	4	4	3%
1	0	2	9	252	46	1	95	19	4	19%
1	0	4	42	78	12	0	24	7	1	4%
2	0	17	23	301	182	2	255	65	3	10%
11	3	34	43	585	208	3	1314	66	8	23%
4	1	13	49	460	241	3	994	68	9	13%
0	0	0	19	1	7	0	2	5	1	4%
3	0	11	40	226	208	1	127	23	3	10%
11	4	21	20	158	35	3	51	29	2	37%
3	0	6	40	256	98	2	65	38	5	12%
0	0	2	17	15	65	2	154	71	6	3%
0	0	5	35	265	68	2	0	34	3	1%
4	1	9	52	255	265	3	21	48	4	13%
2	0	10	42	539	141	3	133	16	10	9%
4	1	34	30	673	250	5	1147	73	3	13%
4	0	13	57	456	240	4	1098	78	5	10%
1	0	3	33	97	4	0	0	1	1	4%

fat - % fat 🦞 Nutritional Summary

fat	sat. fat	protein	carbohy.	sodium	calcium	iron	vitamin A	vitamin C	fiber	% from fat
1	0	5	52	98	130	1	2973	44	5	3 %
4	1	3	28	38	22	1	7	11	2	23 %
8	2	41	12	191	51	2	17	9	1	26 %
4	0	3	52	55	38	1	13	26	7	14 %
1	0	3	15	41	51	1	1452	122	5	13 %
0	0	0	59	30	16	2	137	28	1	1 %
1	0	4	8	186	27	1	135	10	0	5 %
2	0	6	8	217	33	1	4	5	1	28 %
1	0	4	51	345	49	2	368	12	7	4 %
0	0	1	1	106	43	0	80	32	0	11 %
1	0	2	17	205	29	1	686	19	0	12 %
4	1	7	37	74	170	3	57	17	1	16 %
4	1	4	11	136	81	3	738	42	4	45 %
8	3	29	34	486	208	3	1011	34	3	22 %
4	1	4	49	60	94	2	378	33	4	14 %
2	0	4	36	101	36	2	22	5	2	10 %
3	1	5	42	69	145	2	67	7	2	13 %
3	1	21	12	156	104	2	69	42	1	20 %
1	1	5	39	130	76	3	44	50	3	7 %
7	1	32	68	407	150	3	1568	50	8	14 %
6	1	14	70	452	190	3	1563	50	8	14 %
7	2	4	54	77	126	2	173	25	2	23 %
3	1	16	21	506	55	5	102	20	3	18 %
6	3	24	13	139	21	1	9	35	0	25 %
4	1	2	20	105	19	1	22	20	5	33 %
0	0	2	33	62	45	1	2887	33	4	1 %
0	0	3	4	137	111	3	752	31	3	11 %
1	0	4	39	50	24	1	37	45	1	3 %
4	1	22	12	292	50	8	198	32	2	21 %
1	0	3	16	102	35	2	73	27	3	7 %
8	2	40	41	563	52	3	61	4	1	18 %
1	0	9	53	499	129	3	22	23	1	5 %
1	0	3	14	168	49	1	1964	56	6	9 %
1	1	11	14	171	272	1	149	1	0	10 %

fat - % fat ⚓ NUTRITIONAL SUMMARY

Pavlova, about, 184, 195
Peas with potato and onion tart, 24
Pepper[s], see Bell peppers or Chiles
Pepper sauce, about, 50
Philip, King of Spain, 64
Pickled mussels, 187
Pineapple
    about, 125
    crêpes, 149
    curry sauce, with roasted
        chicken, 128
    cutting, 89, 214
    in fruit salad, 179
    in fruit salsa, 133
    in palusamis, 160
    nieve, 89
    sauce, with crêpes, 149
Pinto beans, in watercress soup, 112
Plantain, in palusamis, vegetarian
    option, 160
Plates, 215
Plum[s]
    in mesclun salad with fruit, 103
    sauce with duck breasts, 98
    sauce with meringue islands, 75
Poached eggs Cartagena, 66
Pohole
    ordering, 140, 222
    salad, 141
Poi, about, 138
Poland ethmix, 25
Pomegranate, 141, 222
Poppy seed angel cake, 45
Pork, in posole, 86
Posole, 86
    about, 81
Potato[es], see also Sweet potatoes
    and celery root purée, 102
    and onion tart, 24
    in palusamis, 160
    in taro and chile cakes, 145
Poultry skin, 214
Prawns, see also Shrimp
    in seafood stew, 114
    with oysters, steamed, 202
Project Bush Tea, 51
Pudding
    fungi Foster [cornmeal
        pudding], 59

Pudding [cont.]
    Koko tapioca, 166
Purdy, Susan, 45, 95
Purée press, 133, 211
Red bell pepper[s]
    in vegetable stir-fry, 131
    red pepper soup, 36
    with spiced spinach [vegetarian
        option], 52
    lamb shanks Frenchie, 55
Rice
    black, 72
    brown, fried, 126
    crusts, about, 214
    green bean, pilau, 164
    pilaf, 204
    saffron, 119
    vinegar, about, 141, 222
Rosemary glaze, 24
Saffron
    about, 24, 223
    rice, 119
St. Thomas Island, 49-51, 55
Salad dressing
    for mesclun salad, 103
    for pohole, 141
    papaya seed, 157
    shaker, 211
Salad[s]
    fruit, 179
    island greens, 157
    mesclun, with fruit, 103
    pohole, or sunflower sprout, 141
    spiced spinach with shrimp, 52
    spinner, 211
    string wing bean, 73
    Union Square summer, 22
Salsa
    fruit, 133
    roasted tomato, 118
    strawberry, 29
    with poached eggs, 66
Samoan Islands, 153-56
Sauce[s]
    about, 215
    balsamic, 22
    berry, for cake, 45
    blackberry, with venison, 190
    chile, with broiled shrimp, 83

Sauces [cont.]
    fruit wine dessert, 195
    miso, with tofu and mushrooms,
        143
    pineapple curry, with chicken,
        128
    pineapple, with crêpes, 148
    orange, for cake, 105
    plum, with duck breasts, 98
    plum, with meringue islands, 75
    tamarind, 175
    tomato-jalapeno, 69
Savoiardi
    about, 75, 223
    in meringue islands, 75
Savoy cabbage
    about, 202, 223
    with prawns and oysters, 202
Sea bass
    about, 39, 223
    with mango chutney, 39
Seafood, see also Fish
    kokoda [Fijian ceviche], 173
    prawns and oysters, steamed,
        202
    stew, Ensenada, 114
Serrano chiles
    about, 53, 223
    in spiced spinach and shrimp,
        52
Shanghai ethmix, 142
Shintani, Terry, M.D., 139
Shrimp, see also Prawns
    broiled, with chile sauce, 83
    in kokoda [Fijian ceviche], 173
    spiced, and spinach, 52
Shulterbrandt-Rivera, Gail, 50
Side dishes,
        see also Vegetable side dishes
    black rice, 72
    couscous with peppers, 42
    green bean rice pilau, 164
    saffron rice, 119
    taro and chile cakes, 145
Slimmer skimmer, 211
Slurry
    about, 215
    cup, 212
Smith, Tony, 186

About Graham Kerr

Now a familiar and trusted friend to three generations of home cooks, Graham Kerr is truly an "ambassador of healthy cooking." He is dedicated to serving people who want to make healthy, enjoyable changes in the way they eat and live—the kind of changes that really last. In addition to his writing and culinary development work, he is a popular public speaker and appears regularly on national television and radio programs. He serves as Contributing Editor of *Cooking Light* magazine and is a regular columnist for *Gourmet Retailer*.

He is highly respected within the culinary profession and was invited to be the first visiting professor at the Culinary Institute of America. He continues to visit and teach there regularly.

Kerr has received the James Beard Foundation Award and was appointed to The College of Diplomats of the National Restaurant Association Educational Foundation in 1997. He is active in a number of humanitarian organizations and is particularly interested in those that seek to address problems of world hunger and health. This is his twenty-third book.

About This Book

The fonts used in this book are The Fell Types, from a series of types called Historical Allsorts developed by THE HOEFLER TYPE FOUNDRY [www.typography.com]. They are a digitization of typefaces cut by the Dutchman Peter de Walpergen for the Bishop John Fell of Oxford University Press, c. 1692—among the first "Old Style" types to be made in England. A passage in THE HOEFLER TYPE FOUNDRY catalog best describes them:

In the design of a proper historical interpretation, the designer's intuition is often of greater importance than the historical source itself. In place of the usual process, in which the type designer undertakes an examination of historical materials and creates a studied redrawing, the Historical Allsorts were an experiment to see how successfully a typeface could be 'resurrected' without the introduction of the designer's ideas, instincts and biases. For this series of types, the original sources were scanned at high resolution, and traced algorithmically by software without human intervention: the faces are thus a product of the machine's uninformed guesswork about the shape of the alphabet. The result is a set of digital fonts which preserves the eccentricities of its hot metal forebears, for better or worse—a warmly arrhythmic pace, sometimes unorthodox character sets—overall, they feel agreeably [and ironically] un-digital.

If you are interested in staying in touch with Graham, please let us hear from you! You'll be the first to know about new books, videos, bookstore visits or public appearances that Graham is making in your community. You'll also receive a resource catalog of Graham Kerr's books and tools, including the ones you see pictured in Chapter 14 of this book.

To be included in our mailing list, simply drop us a postcard, return the form below, or visit our web site at www.grahamkerr.com .

Let Us Hear From You!

THE KERR CORPORATION
P. O. Box 1598
Dept. F
Stanwood, WA 98292

EXCLUSIVE OFFER

The Gathering Place Video: $14.95

Follow Graham and Treena as they visit the thirteen ports of call included in *The Gathering Place*. In this one-hour video, you'll hear the sounds and see the sights of markets, gardens, restaurants, and farms they tour. Graham will give you a peek onboard the luxurious Queen Elizabeth II and you'll join him as he interviews chefs, farmers, and market vendors. It's a wonderful keepsake or a thoughtful gift to a "gathering place" friend.

Name _____

Street Address _____

City _____ State/Zip _____

Day Phone _____

Charge to: VISA/ MasterCard _____

Card number: _____ Expiration date: _____

Signature on card _____

Check/money order enclosed for $ _____

The Gathering Place Video—$14.95 each _____

Item #GP-VID   Quantity: _____   Total: _____

_____ Washington residents add 8.6% sales tax: _____

_____ Shipping: _____

_____ Three-day delivery: _____

_____ Total Amount: _____

UPS shipping charges: $35 or less—$5.00, $36 to $60—$7.00
Add $5.00 [in addition to shipping charges] for UPS three-day delivery.
International and Canadian orders: please add $2.00.

Video